Micah Solomon conveys an up-to-the-minute and deeply practical take on customer service, business success, and the twin importance of people and technology.
—**Steve Wozniak,** Apple cofounder

When customers can switch allegiance faster than you can take a breath, there's no more important priority than customer service. Having built several customer service solutions myself, I particularly love Micah's wisdom on what can happen when informed humans and advanced technology such as AI are combined. This is a must-read for any company that wants to differentiate itself.
—**Girish Mathrubootham,** CEO and founder, Freshworks

The service revamp we've undertaken with Micah Solomon and his team has created an elevated level of Member Service that's an essential part of CHROME FCU and our recent and ongoing growth and achievements. In *Can Your Customer Service Do This?* Micah generously shares the secrets that can help readers get started down the same, rewarding path.
—**Robert J. Flanyak,** CPFC, President and CEO, CHROME Federal Credit Union

Micah Solomon's new book *Can Your Customer Service Do This?* is a comprehensive guide that will revolutionize the way you approach customer service. It offers fresh perspectives from a master in this field—and will inspire readers to elevate the level of the service they provide to new heights.
—**Matthias Debecki,** Head of Mergers & Acquisitions, Zech Group SE

Can Your Customer Service Do This? provides a mountain of tips and strategies gleaned from the author's extensive experience. These will help you deliver the customer service and experience that your competitors will only be able to dream of—unless you make the fatal strategic error of sharing your copy of this book with those competitors!
—**Adrian Swinscoe,** *Forbes* contributor, bestselling author, podcast host and producer

CAN **YOUR** CUSTOMER SERVICE

DO THIS?

Create an Anticipatory Customer Experience
That Builds Loyalty Forever

MICAH SOLOMON

New York Chicago San Francisco Athens London Madrid
Mexico City Milan New Delhi Singapore Sydney Toronto

1 2 3 4 5 6 7 8 9   LCR   28 27 26 25 24 23

ISBN   978-1-264-82551-6
MHID   1-264-82551-X

e-ISBN   978-1-264-82638-4
e-MHID   1-264-82638-9

Library of Congress Cataloging-in-Publication Data

Names: Solomon, Micah, author.
Title: Can your customer service do this? : create an anticipatory customer experience that builds loyalty forever / Micah Solomon.
Description: New York : McGraw-Hill Education, [2024] | Includes bibliographical references and index.
Identifiers: LCCN 2023013508 (print) | LCCN 2023013509 (ebook) | ISBN 9781264825516 (hardback) | ISBN 9781264826384 (ebook)
Subjects: LCSH: Customer services. | Customer services—Technological innovations. | Customer loyalty.
Classification: LCC HF5415.5 .S62187 2024 (print) | LCC HF5415.5 (ebook) | DDC 658.8/12—dc23/eng/20230411
LC record available at https://lccn.loc.gov/2023013508
LC ebook record available at https://lccn.loc.gov/2023013509

This publication is designed to provide accurate and authoritative information in regard to the subject matter covered. It is sold with the understanding that neither the author nor the publisher is engaged in rendering legal, accounting, securities trading, or other professional services. If legal advice or other expert assistance is required, the services of a competent professional person should be sought.
—*From a Declaration of Principles Jointly Adopted by a Committee of the American Bar Association and a Committee of Publishers and Associations*

McGraw Hill books are available at special quantity discounts to use as premiums and sales promotions or for use in corporate training programs. To contact a representative, please visit the Contact Us pages at www.mhprofessional.com.

McGraw Hill is committed to making our products accessible to all learners. To learn more about the available support and accommodations we offer, please contact us at accessibility@mheducation.com. We also participate in the Access Text Network (www.accesstext.org), and ATN members may submit requests through ATN.

To my family, friends, colleagues,
and clients: my deepest thanks.

Other books by Micah Solomon

Ignore Your Customers (And They'll Go Away):
The Simple Playbook for Delivering the Ultimate
Customer Service Experience

The Heart of Hospitality:
Great Hotel and Restaurant Leaders Share Their Secrets

High-Tech, High-Touch Customer Service:
Inspire Timeless Loyalty in the Demanding New World
of Social Commerce

Exceptional Service, Exceptional Profit:
The Secrets of Building a Five-Star Customer Service
Organization (coauthored with Leonardo Inghilleri,
Introduction by Horst Schulze)

CONTENTS

FOREWORD

Micah Solomon is a customer service transformation expert, a true artist in this very niche field.

I don't say this lightly—it's not hype or hyperbole. Micah first landed on my radar screen almost 10 years ago, when I was doing research on how companies deliver, or fail to deliver, great customer service. I realized quickly that, while a lot of people talk a big story about delivering great customer service, very few back up that talk with action. While there are lots of reasons for this disconnect, in many cases the problem is they don't know *how* to turn their lofty customer service visions into tangible change throughout their organization.

Micah is one of the very small handful of people who do.

In fact, when I profiled Micah in the pages of *Inc. Magazine*, I proclaimed him "The World's #1 Customer Service Turn-around Expert." And over and over, I've seen just how powerful Micah's approach can be, with all sorts of businesses, in all types of industries.

Transformational, in fact.

There's a reason why Micah is in demand: he's a category of one in the field of customer service transformation—an essential discipline today. Micah offers a lifeline that companies reach for whenever interactions with customers start to go south. And, more positively, when they're ready to turn customer service into a competitive advantage and driver of growth.

When Micah speaks, people listen. And they should.

I confess that I'm a bit jealous of Micah because he seems to have more fun with his job than anyone I've met in a long time. When I see him onsite delivering live training, or on the soundstage filming a customized eLearning training module, or doing anything else that is involved in customer service transformation, it's clear that both he and his audience are having a ball.

One particularly fun part of his work (at least, that's how it looks to me!) is the hands-on mystery shopping that Micah and his talented team undertake at the start of a customer service transformation engagement. This is when Micah and his team literally go undercover, onsite, as part of a current-state analysis of where his client company's customer service experience stands right now.

This means that, on any given day, you could find Micah (or probably *not* find him, as he's pretty good at disguises) "shopping" a bank, car dealership, grocery store, tech startup, or multinational organization.

Or, as in the example you're about to read, one of the world's grandest five-star hotels.

What I've seen over my years covering the business landscape and collaborating with CEOs and other executives at multiple organizations is this: The world is getting more and more commoditized. It's becoming very much a sea of sameness, with customers ever more inclined to switch from one provider to another on little more than a whim.

Yikes! That's not a pretty—or profitable—situation for a company to find itself in. Happily, a direct and lasting way you can distinguish your own business from similar competitors is by delivering great customer service.

Apply the customer service lessons you are about to learn in this book—in every interaction, at every touchpoint—and I promise you that your organization will thrive.

And so will you.

I'll let Micah pick up the story here. I know you're going to enjoy the ride!

Peter Economy
The Leadership Guy at *Inc.* Magazine

INTRODUCTION
The Dream of Perfection

C hances are, my morning started a bit differently from yours. I was undercover, in disguise, performing the mystery review component of a customer service initiative for one of my clients, a famous-name, five-star resort hotel. Going undercover to observe and experience the quality of a client company's customer service is one of the many interesting and enjoyable aspects of my work—if you can even call it *work*—and today I was having a particularly good time.

After a glorious room service breakfast, I headed into the resort's five-star, *Forbes*-rated spa, where I was massaged, manicured, pedicured (that last service was overdue, if you must know), and "facialed" by the spa's exquisitely trained and attentive staff. All the while, I was observing and committing to memory impressions of the customer service/ hospitality behaviors happening all around me: how the spa's employees interacted with the rest of the spa clientele and, of course, how they were treating *me*.

Then, after I recovered from the (nominal!) hardships of my morning activities, I slipped into the hotel's restaurant for lunch, where I similarly sleuthed my way through each phase of the meal. Before I was even seated, I was assessing each customer service touchpoint as it was revealed to me, from the ease of making a reservation to the quality of the hostess's greeting to the dessert presentation to the graciousness with which my final bill was delivered.

And my job wasn't done, yet.

Making today even sweeter was knowing that when night rolled around I'd be snuggling between my guestroom's Egyptian cotton sheets (with a stratospheric thread count, naturally). And that just before I called it a night, I'd be conducting one final, delicious test: a call to room service to see if they could bring me a late-night cup of cocoa in a timely manner and, per my instructions, "not too hot," hoping that request would not devolve into lukewarm or even flat-out cold cocoa, or be overlooked entirely.

Tomorrow, I'll format my confidential report and forward it to the resort's leadership. Since nearly everyone has done their job well during my visit, they're going to like what they read.

And that, I'd say, is a perfect day—because of the spot-on performance of the resort's staff, and because, let's face it, my job can be a *romp*.

Micah in one of his less-subtle disguises.

That's Micah In Disguise. Here's Why.

It's a prickly sensation to spot my own face on a WANTED-style poster pasted on a hotel's valet stand, or on the swinging door of a restaurant kitchen, or at a bank branch on a memo marked "urgent!" that a bank manager has left visible on their desk. It means that word of my work as a customer service transformation expert-slash-Sherlock Holmes has somehow leaked out and spread through the ranks of a company even before I've visited their place of business.

But it's rather missing the point to try to uncover me—to "make" me, as they say on the spy shows—since I only visit a business to help that business improve, rather than to look for "gotcha" moments.

Still, I suppose it's understandable.

So, over time, disguising myself has become more important and my disguises have grown more elaborate. (If you spot someone with Groucho eyebrows and a grease-paint mustache, that's *probably* not me, but it *might* be.)

My work in customer service transformation aims to take a company ever closer to the ideal of customer service perfection. This requires choreographing multiple employee behaviors via training, eLearning, best practices delineation, and a deliberate framework for reinforcement, to create exceptional—spectacular, even—customer service.

In the upcoming pages I'll personally mentor you on how to make such service the norm at your business, customer after customer, interaction after interaction.

Don't worry if you've yet to succeed in providing such an extraordinary level of customer service at your business, or if you haven't figured out how to do so on a consistent basis. We'll get there—together.

Good Enough . . . Isn't

If you've felt instinctively that there's more excellence that can be brought to your organization's customer service experience, that there is an elevated state out there that is achievable (even if most companies in the marketplace don't even try to achieve it), then this book is for you.

This won't be a book about taking shortcuts, or about providing a "good enough" customer experience. (And, candidly, if that's what you're looking for, you should put this book aside until your mood and mindset are ready for a change.)

Instead, it's about going deeper and higher, adding more polish, even some *swagger*, to the the experience you create for your customers.

It's going to be an exhilarating, if strenuous, ride—a ride with phenomenal and company-changing results. You'll be creating as close to a "promised land for customers" as can be achieved, where your employees are mission-driven, empowered, and creative in the solutions they deliver to your customers; where heated moments with customers are rare and easily resolved (and the resulting customer reviews after such resolutions are almost uniformly phenomenal); where your company growth is stimulated day after day by this secret weapon you've now added to your arsenal: a uniquely close connection with an activated and engaged customer base.

What *Is* Customer Service?

Customer service is the assistance an organization provides to those who use its products or services.*

---

* And, occasionally, even the assistance given to those who ultimately *don't* become customers, i.e., when you graciously assist someone on their way to a provider who is more suitable for their needs.

The term can also encompass *internal customer service,* which is a rather beautiful way to describe the assistance and support given by one colleague to another at work.

A related term is *customer experience,* often abbreviated as CX. There are entire essays written on how these two terms—customer service and customer experience—are or aren't synonymous. This debate doesn't interest me much; *of course* you can only provide great customer service if you're providing a great customer experience, and vice versa. So I'm happy to use the two terms interchangeably, depending on context and audience.

Exceptional Customer Service Lets Your Company Escape the Deadly Commodity Zone

In cold, hard business terms, why is delivering exceptional customer service so valuable? Why is it worth the investment when you have other business challenges and opportunities also calling out for attention?

Well, not to go all *Eeyore* on you, but it's highly unlikely that your company or brand offering is entirely unique. Most companies hover a lot closer to the deadly commodity zone than anyone at those companies realize. So, the odds are reasonable that this may include your company as well.

What is the *commodity zone*? It's one of the scariest places for a company to find itself. It's where your business is viewed as more or less interchangeable with the competition, where your current customers are happy to jump ship to one of your competitors, for a myriad of minor reasons:

▶ A slightly lower price
▶ A faster website
▶ A shinier app
▶ A slightly more convenient location

Or, sometimes, for no discernible reason at all.

Happily, there *is* a way you can keep your brand from becoming a commodity—replaceable, interchangeable—in the eyes of the marketplace. Build such a reputation for customer service excellence, and such a strong connection with every customer you touch, that your service becomes a point of distinction, a survival lifeline, and, ultimately, a powerful engine for growth. You may never have to worry about being viewed as a commodity again.

The Long-Term Payoffs from Exceptional Customer Service

An exceptional customer experience will create multiple positive results for your business, most centrally the creation of passionately loyal customers.

Passionately loyal customers are:

▶ Less price sensitive.
▶ More likely to be interested in any new products, services, or brand extensions you may roll out in the future.
▶ More understanding when things go sideways. (This is true. I promise! Once you've done so much, so well,

for your customers, you achieve a state where the little mistakes—and even the occasional massive blunder!—are looked upon in a better, more forgiving, light.)

A loyal customer is also your best form of marketing, bar none. There is nothing more powerful in growing a business than the ambassadorship of customers who are so engaged, so *activated*, that they take on the mission of spreading the good word about your company as crusaders for your brand, who share their passion for your company with their online connections and real-life contacts as well.

. . . And the Personal Benefit You'll Experience Right Away

There's one more benefit that you'll experience immediately as you dig into the work we're going to do together. Even before you achieve the state of customer activation, loyalty, and ambassadorship that I've just promised, the benefits of your new approach will make themselves known to you personally. You'll find yourself shoring up relationships *within* your company, and you'll discover that your own work becomes more pleasant and rewarding.

Who Are You, Micah, to Be Making These Promises?

An exceedingly valid question to be asking, before you commit to spending your time and brain cells with me.

So, here goes:

I've built my reputation client by client and engagement by engagement, working with everyone from small organizations with miniature budgets to some of the world's largest and most respected brands. And I've always done my work with the same aim: to achieve an exceptional level of customer service excellence.

I've written five books on the subject (the one you're reading is my fifth), and I've shared my expertise via *Harvard Business Review*, *Forbes*, *Investor's Business Daily*, the *Los Angeles Times*, the *Washington Post*, the *Atlanta Journal-Constitution*, and on CBS, NBC, and other networks.

I've also involved myself in customer experience technology innovation, including as an early investor in some of the technology included in what we all know and love (or hate) as Apple's Siri, as well as using my own methods to grow my own company, a manufacturing operation that I built up from my spare bedroom to a place of prominence in our field of play, a story known to readers of Seth Godin's landmark book, *Purple Cow*.

Apparently, I Was Born This Way (Maybe You Were, Too)

But it's not only my professional experiences that have brought me to this point. There's a case to be made that I was *born this way*, as a *particularly* particular person when it comes to all things that we now call customer service.

And Here's Some (Reconstructed) Evidence from the Solomon Family Archive

Long ago (I was 11 going on 12), my parents received a letter from my sleepaway camp counselors upon my return from my first summer away. My folks squirreled away that original letter to protect my feelings, but I did manage to see it briefly, and it read something like this:

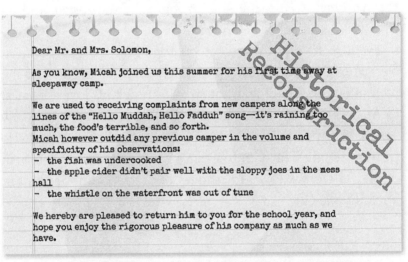

Dear Mr. and Mrs. Solomon,

As you know, Micah joined us this summer for his first time away at sleepaway camp.

We are used to receiving complaints from new campers along the lines of the "Hello Muddah, Hello Fadduh" song—it's raining too much, the food's terrible, and so forth.
Micah however outdid any previous camper in the volume and specificity of his observations:
- the fish was undercooked
- the apple cider didn't pair well with the sloppy joes in the mess hall
- the whistle on the waterfront was out of tune

We hereby are pleased to return him to you for the school year, and hope you enjoy the rigorous pleasure of his company as much as we have.

**Reconstruction of the note Micah's parents
received from his summer camp counselors.**

Oh boy. I must have been an exhausting kid to have at summer camp. Still, I like to think that the very qualities that made me such a trial and tribulation to my camp counselors also make me well suited for the work that now consumes my professional life.

What About You? Are You as Obsessed with Customer Service Excellence as I Am?

Sometimes I meet other people who are likewise obsessed with customer service excellence. Often, they confess this when they come up to meet me after a training or speech or at a book signing. That's where they'll tell me (usually in a quiet voice) some version of the following:

> *I've always been passionate about customer service, but sometimes it feels like I'm the only one. Nobody else seems to care about this stuff the way I do, but I live and breathe it; it's in my bones.*

These customer service enthusiasts span every discipline and industry. They're nurses and administrators in healthcare, tellers and managers at banks, enlisted soldiers and officers in the military, and people serving in our federal, state, and local governments. Including, most recently:

▶ **The banking vice president** who told me, "If it weren't frowned on when I personally take customer support calls, I'd do it every day in a heartbeat. Sometimes I hear such insensitive language used by us on these calls that it sets my teeth on edge."

   (If you share this banker's passion for improving the language we use in conversations with customers, see Chapter 6 for guidance on the proper word choices to make in customer service.)

▶ **The owner-operator of a chain of car washes** who told me, "I'm driven to excellence every day by my awareness that customers *could* just wash their cars at home, when it comes down to it. It's the *experience*, the *something extra* we strive to provide at our car washes that either makes paying for our services worth it or not."

(If you, like this car wash owner, are devoted to providing that *little extra something* for every customer, you can discover how to systemize this via "gold-touch" customer service in Chapter 2.)

► **The manager at a much-beloved retailer** who told me that her own company's famously high service standards are such that it's hard for her to enjoy being a customer anywhere else, because she always finds herself "biting my lip" to avoid sharing unsolicited suggestions when she's supposed to be enjoying herself as a customer.

(For a discussion of customer service standards, with pointers on developing your own, visit the final chapter of this book, Chapter 12. I've also gone ahead and included a hefty helping of such standards throughout this book that you can borrow from me verbatim.)

► **The healthcare administrator** who shared her belief with me that "the consideration and compassion with which we deliver healthcare here makes a tangible difference to the experience of our patients," and, she believes, to the success of their medical outcomes as well.

(If you share this healthcare administrator's interest in consideration and compassion, visit, in particular, Chapter 4.)

> **Note:** If you share this interest in improving the patient experience in healthcare, please send an email with the subject line "Bonus Patient Experience Resource" to health@micahsolomon.com and I will send you my RESPECT Patient Experience Model, along with other patient experience–specific resources. Please also include a sentence or two about who you are, what you do, and what you're facing daily at your work in healthcare!

* * *

All in all, if you are consumed by a desire to create a level of customer service excellence higher than almost anybody else in business even considers to be possible, this book is for you. So, let's dig in and get started.

The Book Club (or Video Club) Method of Finding Your Secret Customer Service Army

If you're feeling alone in your passion for service, it may be helpful and heartening to identify who else in your organization shares this interest, because they may be all around you, hiding in plain sight. A low-risk trick for identifying fellow service enthusiasts in your organization is to start a book club dedicated to the subject. (And how about this for a good deal: If you want to start your club off with the book you're reading right now, and buy book copies from me, I may be able to host a session or two for you for free! Email me at club@micahsolomon.com and let's make it happen!)

Or, if your colleagues aren't particularly book people, make it a video club, featuring and reviewing customer service

videos. (You can visit this page on my site, micahsolomon
.com/training [link is case-sensitive] for a free training video
to get you started.)

**For a look at a training video like the one pictured, visit
micahsolomon.com/training [link is case-sensitive].**

If all this sounds like too much work, you can always
shoot me an email at micah@micahsolomon.com and I'll
sympathize with your customer service passions personally.

Liberties I've Taken in This Book

Anecdotes that feature clients of mine, past or present, have
been altered to make those involved unidentifiable. Locations, brand and personnel names, and the nature of an
industry were all fair game to be tinkered with in the process
of writing this book. I've also used simplification and con-
densation for the sake of making examples clearer and more
useful. Finally, some material in this book is adapted from
my previously published articles.

——— ◄ **CHAPTER 1** ► ———

CLIMBING THE LOYALTY LADDER

Propel Your Organization up the Three Rungs of Customer Service

The way I see it, your decision to read this book already puts you ahead of the game. Here's my logic: there are literally billions of human beings out there who, unlike you, will never read this, or any other book, on the subject of customer service improvement! And because of your demonstrated interest in the subject, I'm going to assume that you're already providing "pretty good, much of the time" customer service. You're *already* getting quite a few things right—at least on most days and in most customer interactions. So, take a moment to pat yourself on the back.*

If I'm right about this, it means that you've already learned the value of customer service from the moments when you

---

* But don't strain your neck.

have gotten it right, and you're now inspired to take these successes even further. You're ready to elevate and polish your relationships with customers to a level sufficient to build the customer connections (and business results) that you've always hoped to achieve.

In other words, you're ready to get out of the middle of the pack—what I call Rung 2 of the Service Level Ladder—and ascend to the top. This middle rung, Rung 2, is where you're judged to be *more or less satisfactory* by your customers, but you're not yet loved (or even probably remembered) for the quality of customer service you provide.

This second rung is, of course, loads better than Rung 1 (unacceptable service), but it's never going to inspire the kind of engagement, passion, and loyalty you need from customers to grow your business.

The problem is that *a merely satisfied (Rung 2) customer will still have a wandering eye.* And how can you blame them? If your more-or-less-decent customer service is no better and no worse than what your competitors are also able to supply, where's the value to a customer limiting themselves to only one supplier—you?

In other words, here's what you need to remember:

A merely satisfied customer belongs to the marketplace.

A loyal customer belongs to you.

This is why it's so important to elevate your organization's performance to Rung 3, the level of truly iconic customer service, where customers now consider you their *only* possible supplier—a category of one—and go out of their way to sing your praises and share the word about the extraordinary level

The Service Level Ladder

(© 2023 Four Aces Inc., Micah Solomon, President)

of customer service you provide. Once you're viewed this way in the marketplace, you'll be able to use your new, elevated status to grow your company reputation and to reliably grow your bottom line.

Becoming Iconic: Moving Your Organization up the Customer Service Ladder

In the upcoming pages, you'll learn the secrets of climbing up the ladder to Rung 3: how to provide personalized, memorable, loyalty-building customer service via elements that include the more or less magic principle of gold-touch customer service (Chapter 2), how to harness the power of recognition (Chapter 4), how to put in place an effective service recovery framework for when things aren't going smoothly (Chapter 5), the right and wrong language to use (Chapter 6), how to deploy customer-focused technology without losing the human touch (Chapter 7), the principles and practicalities of inspiring customer-centric innovation (Chapter 11), and more.

The Art of Anticipatory Customer Service

These elements by and large share one organizing principle: the principle of anticipatory customer service.

Anticipatory customer service means getting to where the hockey puck is headed *before* the puck gets there. It's giving the customer what they want:

> *before* they ask for it,

> *before* they even *know* they want it,

> even if they *never* get around to asking for it.

The *baseline* customer service equation is when a customer asks for something and you provide it to them. This has value, of course, but it's not enough to give rise to special feelings in a customer and to linger in their memory.

But iconic, loyalty-building customer service occurs when you seek out and take care of desires, needs, and questions that a customer has left unexpressed. Customers don't ask for what they need because, among other reasons, they aren't knowledgeable enough to realize that they could benefit from some aspect of your product or service or they don't even know that you can offer it. Or, maybe, they aren't an asser-tive person in public—they don't want to be "too much of a bother." (Yes, such gentle, unassuming customers do exist.)

Anticipatory customer service involves hearing *more* than what a customer says out loud. Uncovering and taking care of unspoken needs and wishes and answering unasked ques-tions is a master principle of service that will bring your company into a new reality: a destination populated with delighted customers who provide you with the kind of loyalty and enthusiastic referrals that will help your company grow and prosper for the long term.

There is nothing more powerful in the world of business.

CLIMBING THE LOYALTY LADDER

Propel Your Organization up the
Three Rungs of Customer Service

The way customer service is delivered in our world ranges from truly amazing to depressingly bad—and a lot that falls in between. To make the delivery of customer service as simple to visualize as possible, I have developed the Service Level Ladder.

The Service Level Ladder has three rungs—the higher your people and your organization climb up the ladder, the better the service they're delivering:

Rung 1. This is the lowest step on the ladder, *unacceptable service*. If your organization is stuck on this rung, you've got your work cut out for you. I'm going to guess, however, that this isn't where you are. Why? You've invested in reading this book, so you already know how much value there is in service.

Rung 2. *Satisfactory service*. Satisfactory service is a big step above unacceptable service. Satisfactory service fulfills the baseline commercial equation: a customer asks for something and you respond by providing it. The problem is that satisfactory customer service can still leave you, in the mind of customers, interchangeable with your competition. It's not enough to create strong customer emotions or keep customers loyal to you; it's not enough to keep them from leaving you for the competition for all sorts of trivial reasons—or for no discernible reason at all.

Rung 3. *Iconic (anticipatory) service.* Rung 3 customer service builds on satisfactory customer service by adding another element: anticipation—hearing (and acting on) *more than what a customer says out loud.* This is where you give customers what they want:

> *before* they ask for it,
>
> *before* they even know they want it,
>
> even if they never get around to asking for it.

When you master this level of service, it becomes a loyalty-building, competitive advantage that will grow your business customer by customer, year after year.

CHAPTER 2

GOLD-TOUCH CUSTOMER SERVICE

A Loyalty-Building Practice Anyone Can Master

Feeling the ever-more insistent tug of nature, but not wanting to leave my laptop unattended for even a minute,* I asked my server at the five-star Madera restaurant in the heart of Silicon Valley,

> *"How comfortable should I feel leaving my laptop on the table while I step out for a minute?"*

> ***"Very** comfortable," she answered, "because I will be here with it,"*

---

* One of the things that made my laptop so precious that day was that it contained an early manuscript of the book you're now reading!

moving into an arms-crossed, standing-guard position like a sentry at the Tower of London that she was still maintaining (with perhaps a bit of humorous exaggeration) when I returned.

What the well-trained server, Audrey Boisvert, was practicing was *gold-touch customer service.*

Gold-touch customer service comes in two varieties. The first is the *do-extra*: giving a customer more effort than they've asked for or could reasonably expect. The second is the *tell-extra*: providing a customer with unexpected, additional value by answering a question with particular thoroughness or by making a connection with a customer on a human, shared passion level.

If you want to transform your company's relationship with customers, I encourage you to practice gold-touch customer service whenever you find or can create a do-extra or tell-extra opportunity. It's a simple practice that can enrich customer interactions and elevate how customers think of your business.

Gold-Touch Examples in Various Industries and Contexts

In the examples of gold-touch customer service that follow, you'll notice they generally aren't massive, splashy, scene-stealing gestures. Yet each one is more than enough to distinguish a company from its competition, brighten a customer's day, and put that customer one step closer to true brand loyalty.

Do-extras:

▶ An auto dealership employee could pair a customer's cellphone to their new car's system *before* they drive off the lot, rather than allowing them to drive away only to get frustrated (and perhaps even into a fender bender) while trying to handle it themselves on the road.

▶ A hair salon employee could run out and feed the parking meter for an arriving client so they don't have to fumble around trying to find change.

▶ A clothing salesperson at a department store could send Girl Scout cookies in the mail to a customer who has mentioned a weakness for, say, Thin Mints (that's me!) or Caramel deLites (that's me when Thin Mints aren't available). My salesperson at Nordstrom, in fact, does this. (She's the fabulous Joanne Hassis at Nordstrom's King of Prussia, Pennsylvania, location.)

Tell-extras:

▶ A paralegal could respond to a first-time legal services client who asks about hours of operation with, "The building is open from 8:30 a.m. until 7:00 p.m.," (Here, they've answered the question the client *actually* asked.) "and you'll want to head to the last bank of elevators to access the higher floors, including ours." (Here, they've added a valuable tell-extra.)

▶ Someone scheduling or confirming an appointment for a job applicant—yes, in many senses, job applicants are customers, too!—could volunteer, "Your interview is at 9 a.m.," (This answers the applicant's expressed question.) "and be sure to bring your driver's license to get into the building—they can be sticklers for that downstairs." (This provides a useful tell-extra that may head off later frustration.)

▸ A cashier at the checkout line could admire—sincerely—one of the articles a customer is purchasing. (This one requires nuance. Trader Joe's is both by and large great at this and occasionally mocked for sometimes appearing to do this by rote.)

▸ A company that sells a potentially confusing product could include helpful, very specific links, or even—and this is one of my favorites—a brief and highly personalized introductory tutorial video. (The flip side of this is that you need to curate what you send. Too much information, à la the final archives scene in *Raiders of the Lost Ark*, is nearly as unhelpful as too little.)

One of the Most Powerful Kinds of Gold-Touch . . .

. . . at least of the tell-extra variety, is when you're able to make use of a distinctive nugget of information that you've picked up about a particular customer. This kind of detail is often right there and ripe for the taking, but you need to have your ears perked up, your eyes open, and your antennas, so to speak, extended. These nuggets can be a customer's hobbies, recreation choices, love of dogs or cats (or their revulsion thereof), food or beverage preferences, and the neighborhood where they live; as well as, more seriously, details like food allergies, challenges with low vision, physical mobility (disability) issues,* and the like.

Always be on the lookout for these one of a kind gems.

Like Any Good Deed, Gold-Touch Has the Potential to Backfire

Watch out for these common gold-touch pitfalls:

▸ Resist the impulse to offer personalization based on information that the customer will feel uncomfortable knowing that you have. The front desk manager of a hotel shouldn't call a guest in their room and try to gold-touch them by offering an exclusive bourbon tasting based on "how much you've enjoyed the miniature bottles of liquor in your minibar." Yes, things like this *do* happen. No, this isn't a way to endear yourself to your guests.

▸ Avoid basing a gold-touch on information that was confidentially shared with you or shared as a requirement of service. While a customer will understand your need to ask their date of birth for legitimate compliance reasons, if you then use it as a public marketing vehicle via LinkedIn postings or unsolicited postcards, it may not be appreciated.

▸ Avoid basing a gold-touch on anything that comes too close to an obvious danger area, like religion or politics.

---

* Although disability-related provisions should be considered part of the *standard* service we all provide, I'm putting them in the gold-touch category because, in practice, they are rarely given proper consideration by most service providers. Please be the exception.

Be Gentle with Your Employees If Their Early Gold-Touch Efforts Go a Little Sideways

Be careful to avoid quashing the tender efforts of employees who are just learning the art of providing gold-touches. Searching for opportunities and then delivering gold-touches is a mindset, a behavior, and eventually, if all goes well, a habit. But as with anything creative and personal, it can be tricky to get exactly right. Most commonly, when an employee is starting out, they'll be too overbearing or too personal; alternatively and not as commonly, they may be a little one-size-fits-all in their approach.

If employees start feeling defeated and begin tying themselves into knots with the fear that their gold-touch attempts won't meet your high standards, then the habit is unlikely to take root and flourish. Everyone in leadership positions should take pains to *applaud* rather than *criticize* employees who go about their do-extras or tell-extras in a different way from how they imagine they would have handled things themself. And remember: whenever an employee is diverted from their regularly scheduled activities to provide gold-touch customer service that couldn't be planned for in advance, it isn't fair to give them grief about the regularly scheduled work they weren't able to accomplish during that time.

With a Gold-Touch, It's the Thought That Counts (At Least to Some Extent)

Here's another reason you shouldn't fret if a gold-touch isn't perfectly designed and executed: there's a significant element of "it's the thought that counts, and that sure was thought-ful!" credit that customers will give a business for making a gold-touch effort regardless—well, *almost* regardless—of the grace or awkwardness with which it was executed.

In addition, providing a gold-touch will telegraph to the customer that you're up for handling other forms of assistance they may need in the future. In other words, the more you provide gold-touch service, the more you become *their* provider, and the more closely the customer feels engaged and aligned with you.

Gold-Touch Doesn't Always Have to Be Hand-Crafted and Spontaneous

Although the most meaningful gold-touch gestures are specific and applicable only to the customer to whom they're offered (because they're based on an employee's knowledge of, and cues picked up from, that specific customer), a gold-touch doesn't always have to be as personal and spontaneous as all that. Choreographed, scripted, universally applicable gold-touches can have value, too:

- ▶ The pet grooming outfit that sends every customer home with a blue or pink bandana around its neck* after making it through its grooming ordeal.
- ▶ The car dealership that puts a bottle of chilled water in the cupholder of every car after service, to be discovered by the driver upon exit. (The environmentalist in me offers this example with some hesitation.)

---

* Its furry customer, that is, not its human customer—except, I suppose, upon request!

▶ The theme park where every employee, whether a groundskeeper or an executive, knows to drop their assigned tasks and jump to:

- Offer directions any time they see a guest beginning to unfold their theme park map.
- Offer to take a photo when they see a family group forming for a selfie that will be improbably large and neck-and-shoulder straining unless taken by someone *not* in the group.

Just keep in mind that, on the one hand, these choreographed, preplanned gold-touches have the potential to reach the largest number of customers, on the other hand, they tend to lose their impact over time as they become an *expectation* rather than an extra.

On the *other* other hand, you may be fortunate enough to have a choreographed gold-touch become a brand trademark and attraction, as the chocolate chip cookies at DoubleTree hotels have become. Now how cool would *that* be?

Seriously Now, Micah, How Am I Expected to Find Time for This?

I can picture your eyes rolling as you've been reading this, thinking, "sure, sure, whatever you say, Micah, but fumbling around for opportunities to gold-touch our customers is the *last* thing anyone at my company has time to squeeze in to their already busy days!"

Well, good point. Forget everything you've just read.

Just kidding.

While more elaborate gold-touches do take time, if you don't have time for those yet,* there are still, in my experience, opportunities that will arise for gold-touches that are ripe for easy plucking, so long as you have a gold-touch mindset and are paying even a smidgeon of attention:

- ▶ Any time something doesn't go as well as expected, you have a chance to go the extra mile in a gold-touch sort of way. Let's say you're a security company that had to delay installation due to an unexpected room layout idiosyncrasy within a customer's house. In this case, you could do something as simple as working closely with the customer to conveniently reschedule the updated installation.

- ▶ Any time something goes right (e.g., when a customer of the security company volunteers how happy they are to *finally* have the right system installed after the miseries of working with prior vendors) you also have a chance to add a gold-touch, whether it's simply expressing to the customer your happiness at hearing their thanks, or sending them a card congratulating them on their new success.

- ▶ Any time a customer neglects to ask for something that you, in your professional judgment, know they would benefit from. This could be, for example, recommending that a customer add water leak sensors to their security system, a solution that could, as you explain to the customer, "save you from thousands of dollars in financial losses and weeks of inconvenience while the water damage is repaired." And while this *could* be considered an upsell, if it's a thoughtful and appropriate recommendation, most customers won't see it that way.

---

* I predict you will start to *make time* once you see how effective gold-touching is.

Even a Funeral Can Benefit from a Choreographed Gold-Touch

I have found that the funeral industry ("deathcare," as it is sometimes called) often attracts particularly customer-focused personnel to its ranks. The majority of funeral directors and their staff are attuned to what can impact their grieving customers and will respond by doing whatever it takes to make their customers comfortable, as in the following instance.

While grief may be the overarching emotion for adults after a loss, hunger can strike almost as acutely when you're a child.

"My kids and I had run out of the house early the morning of my father's [the children's grandfather's] funeral without eating much," a mom tells me. "As a result, on the way to the gravesite for burial, after having already made it through the morning viewing, my kids were getting hungry and well on the way to *hangry*.

"Then, a godsend happened on the way to the limousines: the funeral professionals handed each of us a brown bag of buttered bagels and bottles of water. I'll never forget their kindness and forward thinking."

How to Create an Environment Where Gold-Touch Behavior Will Flourish

As I've been emphasizing, your goal should be to create an environment and culture where gold-touch behavior becomes the norm. Here are my suggested ways to accomplish this:

▶ **Build gold-touch into your customer service training.**
Gold-touch is a principle that should be routinely
taught and retaught in your customer service trainings.
(See the "Two Free Gold-Touch Tools for My Readers"
callout for how to access my eLearning training video
on gold-touch for free.)

Two Free Gold-Touch Tools for My Readers

1. I encourage you to email me for a private link (on your
   honor to keep it private) to my eLearning training video
   on gold-touch at goldtouch@micahsolomon.com.
2. For a standalone, printable version of my Gold-Touch
   Prompts to Get You Started, email me at prompts@
   micahsolomon.com and I'll hook you up right away.
   Please take a moment in your email to tell me about
   your situation, company, and yourself!

▶ **Make gold-touch part of employee onboarding
(orientation).** It's never too early for an employee to
learn about gold-touch. Start on day one.
▶ **Lead by example.** Provide gold-touches to customers
yourself. Do so especially when you know employees are
watching. (Your secret is safe with me!)
▶ **Celebrate gold-touches and those who provide
them.** When you catch employees engaging in gold-
touch behavior, recognize (and maybe even reward)
them right then and there. Also, take the time to

systemically build ways to celebrate these efforts on your physical or virtual bulletin board, your internal newsletter, at company events, and elsewhere.

▶ **Empower employees to step out of their planned routines to offer gold-touches as needed.** If employees are always on edge, worrying that management will later reprimand them for having stepped away from scheduled tasks to provide a gold-touch to a customer, they will never feel safe offering gold-touches.

▶ **Build breathing space into employee schedules.** Being *theoretically empowered* to creatively provide gold-touch moments—but *in reality* lacking the time to actually carry them out—isn't a winning combination.

Gold-Touch Prompts to Get You Started

Do-extra:

- Are there preferences your customer has exhibited in the past that you can fulfill now? (Bring them a Diet Coke while they're waiting if they asked for one last time, avoid the standard plastic wrap on your product if they asked you to leave it off on a past visit, etc.)
- Is there something you can add to what you're selling that the customer would appreciate, without it breaking the bank for you (e.g., throwing in an extra blueberry muffin when they order a dozen)?
- Is there additional effort you can provide that the customer would appreciate (for example, walking them to their car while holding an umbrella for

them on a rainy day, or walking around from behind the retail cash wrap counter to hand them their purchases from a side-by-side vantage point)?
- Is there a chance for you to do something that's not exactly within the scope of your business that a customer could benefit from nonetheless?

Tell-extra:

- Interests: hobbies, pets, kids, sports teams, etc.
- Something the customer might benefit from knowing (for example, "You'll want to have a screwdriver bigger than X on hand before you start assembling your new purchase") beyond the generic instructions the manufacturer includes with your product.
- Any time a customer neglects to ask for some information that you, in your professional judgment, think they would benefit from.

* * *

I can't pretend—and neither should you—that gold-touches take zero time. But I would argue that gold-touches ultimately take *less* time than the hours of prospecting you'd otherwise need to replace customers who have drifted away from your company because they weren't touched by you in this loyalty-building way. And the marketing value of gold-touched customers spreading the word to others about their delightful experience with your company is truly beyond measure.

GOLD-TOUCH CUSTOMER SERVICE

A Loyalty-Building Practice Anyone Can Master

G old-touch customer service is a simple practice that can quickly elevate how customers think of your business. Gold-touch comes in two varieties:

Do-extra: When you give a customer more of your effort than they've asked for or would reasonably expect.

Tell-extra: When you provide customers with additional value by answering questions in a particularly thorough way or by connecting with customers on a human, shared passion level.

Often, the best kind of tell-extra is when you make use of a particular tidbit of information that you've picked up about a particular customer. The secret to finding these nuggets is to have your ears perked up, your eyes open, and your antennas, so to speak, extended throughout your day as you interact with customers.

Remember

Gold-touch customer service takes time to learn and often takes employees away from their regular duties. Leaders should applaud gold-touch efforts that their employees make, rather than coming down on employees for having temporarily stepped away from their regular work.

Successfully Delivering Gold-Touch Customer Service Takes Practice

Likewise, leaders should go easy on employees who don't get gold-touch customer service exactly right the first time. You don't want them to be afraid to attempt gold-touch service in the future because you chastised them when their early efforts were delivered awkwardly as they learned the ropes.

CHAPTER 3

THE POWER OF PURPOSE

How to Drive Iconic Customer Service

Let's focus for a moment on one employee: a groundskeeper on the campus of a technology company, starting her workday early in the morning.

The *functional* item on the groundskeeper's to-do list that she was intending to get done this morning? Plant tulips bulbs—two cartons' worth, 200 bulbs in all.

That is, until she noticed a small sinkhole—not huge, but big and deep enough to turn an ankle—right in the middle of the gravel path the company's clients, vendors, and employees will be walking on later in the day as they make their way between buildings on the company's campus.

Here's What Purpose-Driven Behavior Looks Like

At this point, the groundskeeper has two options:

Option 1: She can stay focused on accomplishing her functional, prescribed task, that is, plugging away on planting those tulip bulbs all morning long.

Option 2: Now that she's discovered this safety risk, she can find some spare soil and start filling in the sinkhole before anybody's ankle gets turned.

Of course, Option 2 sounds great on paper, but is the employee really going to make that choice? *Don't be so sure.*

Consider: There's no manager nearby to approve this improvised, potentially ankle-preserving decision. If the groundskeeper decides to deviate from her prescribed routine for the sake of future pedestrians, she'll have to make that decision for herself, in the face of her existing obligation to get all 200 bulbs into the ground by the end of the morning. So, in a typical, check-off-that-checklist organization, the groundskeeper's best option, if she wants to avoid career-harming repercussions, is to stick to planting those bulbs.

However, if she's a *purpose-driven employee working for a purpose-driven organization,* she can choose to temporarily pull herself away from her assigned duties without worrying about the repercussions if she doesn't get all 200 bulbs into the ground before noon.

With her *sense of purpose* prompting her to do so, she'd be taking care of the comfort and safety of clients, vendors, and her fellow employees—something that her purpose-driven organization would encourage and applaud.

Function Versus Purpose

Sparking this kind of mindset and behavior in any organization requires creating an environment in which every employee understands that "my typical, day-to-day *function* here may be to [plant tulip bulbs, park cars, answer the phone, schedule appointments, etc.], but my *purpose* is to _____."

The Necessity of Unlocking Your Employees' Elective (Optional) Efforts

When an employee engages in something like repairing a walking path *before* an ankle is turned or broken (or searching out and anticipating unspoken customer desires, or otherwise being creative in ways that are essential to moving your company up to the "iconic" rung of the service ladder) they're gifting your company and gracing your customers with their elective (optional) efforts.

Elective efforts are behaviors that are done (or avoided) at the sole discretion of the doer. And it's upon these elective efforts that customer service excellence (and, more broadly, organizational excellence) depends.

The thing is, a leader or manager can't simply *force* elective behaviors on an employee if the employee is not willing to play along. Because when an employee is uninspired and disengaged, they can actually be quite resourceful at keeping their visible job performance *just above* the line where the boss would hear about it or where the employee might be hauled in by HR for a performance improvement plan. As a result, no matter what you pay them—and no matter how hard you think you're working them—they're never going to give you the extra-mile behaviors that serve your customers in a loyalty-building way *unless they choose to.*

So, since you can't force or pay an employee to provide elective efforts, you're going to need to find other ways to unlock their desire to contribute.

The first step to take: Get clear on the principle you want to use to guide employees in their work. This means *codifying* (spelling out) your intended organizational purpose in a simple sentence—or, at most, two or three sentences—and then internally publicizing this purpose any way you can.

What you're looking to spell out here is *the reason that every person in the organization performs their day-to-day job functions* and *the reason they may need to stray from, or go beyond, those assigned job functions* to provide superior, anticipation-informed customer service.

Creating and publicizing a purpose sentence or short set of sentences might seem like a small step, but it's an essential step as you start your journey toward Rung 3, iconic customer service.

Here's why:

- The power of human beings who understand the reasoning behind their work is *enormous.*
- This same understanding will guide employees in how to behave in any unplanned moment that calls for them to use their discretion in deciding to deviate from their assigned, functional tasks in a way that stays true to the purpose of their work in the organization. (Such would be the case if our groundskeeper does in fact make the decision to break her routine and protect campus walkers.)

What Should Your Purpose Sentence or Sentences Be?

Sorry, that would be cheating for me to choose one for you. This is something you need to create for yourself, or it won't really be yours.

But I'm happy to give some direction and examples to start you on your way.

If you're aiming to unlock the efforts and passion of your staff in a customer-focused way, your purpose statement could be similar to one of the following:

"Our purpose is . . .

". . . to support our healthcare mission by easing the path for every patient and family member we come into contact with" (for a healthcare organization)

". . . to serve our customers as they would wish to be served, during every mile of their automotive journey" (for an automobile retailer)

". . . to delight our customers and assist them with even their unspoken needs and wishes when furnishing their office or home" (for a residential and commercial furnishings company)

Please take note of how *concise and readable* these statements are. Avoid drafting something so long and full of puffery that it's destined for a dusty, unexamined life hidden away inside a drawer or filing cabinet. I expect you know the kind of nonsense I'm referring to: "We aim to architect the most actionable, best-in-class assistance for our multifaceted stakeholders, within our given competencies, in keeping with the realities of current market conditions . . ." Oh boy.

Once you've spelled out your organizational purpose, it's time to get to work conveying it across your business. This will be both an immediate and ongoing challenge, something you'll need to continue to nurture throughout the life of your organization. Here are some suggestions:

▶ **Build philosophical, purpose-focused material into your customer service training program.** While it's true that your customer service training program needs to cover the functional, day-to-day, nuts-and-bolts tasks, best practices, and tricks of the trade involved in delivering exceptional customer service, this training should be be framed and grounded by an explanation of *why* you are doing all of this in the first place.

▶ **Build purpose-focused inspiration into the onboarding (orientation) experience you provide for new employees.** At too many companies, the new employee experience is so awash in competing priorities from the legal department, loss prevention, and so on,* that they take away from what should be a central focus: the seriousness with which your company takes its pro-customer mission and how central that mission is to the work these new employees will be performing.

▶ **Celebrate great customer service moments when they happen.** I'm not talking about direct financial rewards; I'm talking about celebrations of service that has been

---

* Of course, these are important as well. Just don't let them overwhelm and drown out the "purpose" part of your messaging.

well provided. These can be as simple as a personal thank-you to an employee from a manager or letters of appreciation from customers that are posted to the bulletin board, newsletter, or internal website.

I suggest you *systematize* the celebration along the lines of what has worked for years—decades, actually—for the Ritz-Carlton Hotel Company. Twice a week (Monday, to start off the week, and Friday, to bring it to a close), every Ritz-Carlton hotel and resort shares a "wow story" of over-and-above hospitality from one of its more than 100 properties as a way to celebrate such service and disseminate the best-of-the-best creative actions taken on behalf of a hotel's guests. This inspires other employees to greater heights, both through the creative examples shared and through the opportunity to one day have their own moment of "wow" shared and celebrated similarly.

▶ **Strive to involve your entire employee base in efforts toward customer-focused *innovation*.** Once employees understand their purpose in your organization, most will get excited about contributing in ways outside their daily, assigned roles. So, *let them*. If they believe they have found a better way to serve customers (or to support other employees in their customer-serving roles), be sure you have a framework that embraces such contributions. (See Chapter 11 for a discussion of innovation.)

The Limits of Purpose

Every employee will actually have multiple purposes for being at work. Apart from their commitment, ideally, to their organization's purpose once it's been shared with them, they'll also have personal goals that drive them. These include such things as feeding their family, nurturing their private ambitions, and keeping the lights on at home and a full tank of gas (or a charged battery) in their car.

This is something worth acknowledging to yourself and others rather than believing and/or implying that these other purposes need to be quashed in service of the central organizational purpose you're striving to convey. In other words, the single-mindedness of being purpose-driven doesn't need to be in opposition to an employee's personal purposes. Selflessness isn't required here for success.

*   *   *

Empowerment: A Driving Force Behind Exceptional Customer Service

You're going to move a lot further a lot more quickly toward being an organization where purpose-driven employees contribute their elective efforts if you get serious about employee empowerment.

Exceptional customer service requires *room for interpretation* with talented, well-trained, fully empowered employees serving as the interpreters—those who decode and manifest what exceptional customer service *really* looks like in action.

And if they lack empowerment—power, really—they'll remain hobbled, no matter how good their intentions.

Here's how Sam Patel, a hospitality veteran in greater Jacksonville, Florida, explains this:

> *Once your team's assembled, trained, and indoctrinated in the essentials of your philosophy, you have to avoid the mistake of pulling the leash so tight that they can't do their best work for you and for the customer. You have to trust your employees to strive, in their own style, to bring the benefits of hospitality to your customers to the very best of every employee's ability.*

When a leader encourages pro-customer efforts, most everything else will fall in place, with employees eagerly contributing their elective efforts time and again. Conversely, if a company's leadership *doesn't* provide such encouragement and leeway—if it rules with excessive rigidity—these unyielding ways will, over time, blight your organization in the eyes of its customers. An employee cannot fully contribute to an organization and the service of its customers without being empowered.

Need more proof that empowerment is essential for superior customer service? Consider these points:

- ▸ It's impossible for a supervisor or manager to be present at every moment to guide customer interactions.
- ▸ Likewise, a checklist or "thou shalt/shalt not" list of commandments (i.e., "best practices") can't come anywhere close to covering all possible eventualities. Even if it could, it wouldn't be able to do so with the same kind of nuance as a human being who is

face to face or on the telephone with a customer. In other words, an empowered employee is the only force that can be agile—that can adjust in real time (or better than real time, if they're being anticipatory) to what a customer needs or hopes for in the moment.

▶ Empowerment is essential for bringing a purpose-driven culture to life. Without empowerment, you're giving mixed messages: on the one hand, instructing your employees to pursue a pro-customer purpose, but on the other, not giving them the power to do so.

▶ Empowerment is a remarkable human development tool. How can an employee ever know—and how can the leader of that employee ever know—what that employee is capable of until they're given the leeway to demonstrate their potential?

It's an Employee's *Job* to Be Empowered

Since the term "empowerment" became the buzziest of buzzwords, some companies seem to think empowerment—or at least lip service that features the word—is something they can sprinkle atop an otherwise hollow culture and magically get results in a pixie dust fashion. But empowerment needs to be something a company's leadership believes in, embraces, practices, and does everything it can to embed within the company culture.

If you do believe in employee empowerment, one of the keys to conveying this is to make it clear that it is not in fact an add-on, a nice-to-have-sometimes kind of thing. Instead, empowerment is *every employee's job.*

By extension, this means that *it's every employee's obligation to make use of their empowerment,* day in and day out. Which turns it into a powerful force indeed.

Letting go of the reins and handing them off to employees is indisputably hard. But there's no way around it. Empowering employees is absolutely necessary to achieve iconic, Rung 3 customer service—and it will profoundly contribute as well to employee morale, retention, and recruitment.

THE POWER OF PURPOSE

How to Drive Iconic Customer Service

E xceptional customer service depends on becoming a *purpose-driven organization,* the kind of organization where every employee understands that "while my typical, day-to-day *function* may be to [plant tulip bulbs, park cars, answer the phone, schedule appointments, etc.], my *purpose* is to _____."

Defining Your Purpose

The first step toward this understanding is to define your organizational purpose.

Your purpose should be stated as a brief sentence (or, *at most,* two or three sentences) in simple, easy-to-grasp language rather than consultantese or corporate jargon.

Here's an example for an auto parts store:

"Provide the best possible experience while fulfilling all of our customers' automotive needs."

Once you've taken care of this, amplify your purpose every way you can:

- Include your purpose in your training program so employees know *why* they are doing their jobs in the first place—and when it is necessary to step away from what is typically defined as their day-to-day job (their functional tasks).

- Make your purpose a central focus of your new employee onboarding (orientation) process.
- Celebrate customer service triumphs. Let everyone in the company know what kind of behavior is admired.
- Promote customer service innovation. Make sure your employees know you want them to discover new and creative ways to serve customers.

Empower Your Employees

It's impossible to predict every possible scenario in advance or what will work best as a response when a scenario occurs. Instead, an organization needs to be able to depend on employees who are well trained and empowered to deliver Rung 3 customer service.

Strive to have everyone think of empowerment not as an add-on, but like this: *It is an employee's job to be empowered and to make use of that empowerment every day.* It is leadership's job to *support* empowerment, even to the point of applauding an employee who used their empowerment in a way that didn't entirely work out.

CHAPTER 4

THE POWER OF RECOGNITION

Put the Mrs. Gold Principle to Work

For years, I led a domestic manufacturing company that I'd started in the spare bedroom of my tiny house. Over time, it grew to prominence in our modest niche in the marketplace.

Making this growth trajectory more fun, we always had our share of colorful customers with picturesque hobbies, side gigs, and personal passions: Jeremy, the part-time rodeo star; Jessica, who worked weekends as a costumed character at the local theme park (and always dared us to guess which of the theme park's characters was her); Julian, an amateur hypnotist and aspiring life coach; and, finally, Mrs. Gold, the unforgettable customer who will be the star of this chapter.

Back when my company was still tiny, every member of my little team of employees was personally acquainted with

Mrs. Gold* and her endless ability to find a place in her home for *just one more* stray feline in need. So any time Mrs. Gold called us (typically to check on the progress of one of her manufacturing orders), we would greet her amiably, without prompting, by acknowledging and inquiring about her passion for cats.

(Photo credit: Noah Solomon)

As my company grew to include more, and newer, employees, we had to get more systematized if we were going to continue to provide personal recognition to customers like Mrs. Gold, as well as all our other always-unique customers. We pulled this off with a combination of technical pizzazz and manual work, entering colorful details about each customer into our customer relationship management (CRM) system whenever we had a spare moment.

---

* None of these client names are real, not that any of them would really mind.

This way, even after years of company expansion, *anyone* who answered the phone would be cued to offer some variant of, in the case of our favorite cat lady:

> *"Oh, Mrs. Gold! I was **just** thinking about your collection of cats. Are you holding steady at 12 cats . . . or have you perhaps gotten up to . . . 13?"*

I expect that this sounds over the top when you're reading it here in black and white. It's a little farfetched to believe that whatever random employee picked up the phone had Mrs. Gold's collection of cats on their mind the very moment she called in.

However, consider this: Mrs. Gold *herself* would most likely be thinking about her cats any time of the day, including when she called us to check on a project. So the idea that *we* would be thinking about her cats and, by extension, her, would sound eminently reasonable to Mrs. Gold herself. And by aligning our viewpoint with hers, we could continue to provide the kind of recognition that builds a customer for life.

It's Not Just Mrs. Gold; It's (Nearly) Everybody

Whenever we acknowledged Mrs. Gold's assorted felines, we fulfilled her desire for recognition: for being seen, figuratively as well as literally. Almost every human, including the humans we call customers, desires recognition. Customers want us to see them and value them as one of a kind human beings.

So, although no customer is ever going to belly up to the service counter at your business and say, "I want to be recognized by you as the unique and valuable human being I am," customers, with few exceptions, share this desire to be seen, acknowledged, and appreciated.

And when you fulfill this desire, it becomes a powerful (although unspoken and likely unconscious) reason for customers to continue to do business with your company, time after time and year after year after year.

Every Customer Is at the Center of Their Own World

The person a customer cares most about (at least when conducting business with you) is themself. They don't care about, or at least don't give any thought to, the challenges that an employee serving them may be navigating. They don't care that there are other customers who also need to be served, or about the behind-the-scenes realities at your business, least of all your company's organizational chart. (If you want your customer interactions to quickly go awry, *just try* to school your customers on which department provides which services—and why your department *isn't* the right one to provide the customer what they need right now.)

In your customers' day-to-day lives, when they're *not* buying from or being served by you, they may be the most open-hearted, considerate, even philanthropic people in the world. Yet, as customers, they're almost universally focused on themselves (as well as, perhaps, their kids, pets, partner, or, if they're buying for their company in a B2B context, their boss).

A charitable way to put this? It's not that your customers don't care. Rather, they simply *don't realize* that any extraneous (to them) elements and challenges are involved in serving them. From the viewpoint of your customers, while doing business with you, *they* are at the center of the world.

My suggestion is that, rather than resenting this reality, lean into it by *making the customer feel that they're at the center of **your** world as well*. Revamp your attitude by recognizing that embracing your customers' self-focused reality isn't a negative; it isn't demeaning. Instead, it's *a way to get the cash registers to ring*.

Does Putting the Customer in the Center Mean Moving the Employee Out of the Center?

The short answer is "no!"—though this is certainly one of the ways I worry that my teachings will be misapprehended and misapplied.

The longer answer: learning to look through a customer-focused lens when you are providing customer service is entirely compatible with having a company that is focused—in a broader sense—on the needs and aspirations of its employees.

Customer focus shouldn't be used as rationale for unpaid overtime, unfeeling scheduling practices, or HR trickery couched as pro-customer decision-making.

Happily, most pro-customer organizations are also pro-employee.* Why? Multiple reasons: the overall health of most pro-customer organizations; the empowerment

---

* Though, sadly, not all.

employees tend to have there; and the happy phenomenon that when such companies deploy pro-customer efforts, it's nearly inevitable that such efforts will positively affect how a company treats employee needs and aspirations as well.

Serve One Customer at a Time

If you want each customer to feel like they're at the center of your world, learn to focus your attention on just one customer at a time.

Here's the mantra that should be seared into the soul of every employee in an organization:

The only customer who matters is the one who's in front of me right now.

Strive to bring a laser-like focus to the customer who is in front of you (or on the telephone or video call), and let the rest fade into the background.

I can't pretend that focusing on one customer at a time is going to be easy. In any business, there will always be competing priorities and multiple customers clamoring for attention. Nevertheless, making a focused connection with one person, even briefly, is supremely powerful. On the front lines, this power is self-evident. In the back office it's powerful as well, leading to less abrupt communications and correspondence. And in leadership or strategic positions, it keeps you from so completely aggregating how you look at customer feedback and data that you miss the nuances of what *individuals* are asking of you.

Eight Simple Ways to Show Recognition and Put the Customer at the Center of Your World

Providing recognition isn't always a high-wire act. Some of it comes down to practicing positive behaviors until they become second nature. Here are eight simple ways to get started:

1. Use your customer's name. (Within reason! Don't overdo this and start sounding like those irritating fill-in-the-blank salespeople.)

2. Offer the customer *your* name.

3. If a customer takes the time to ask, "How are you doing?," answer them and volley the question back to them: "I'm doing great! And how are *you*, [Jeremy]?"

4. If you know where a customer lives (it's quite possibly included right there on the invoice filling your screen) and you're familiar with the area, comment on how it's a nice or convenient area, that you used to live there, that your daughter lived there when she went to college, etc. (I wouldn't do this, however, with a high-net-worth individual [HNWI] or celebrity—going on about how luxe their neighborhood is may make you sound a bit creepy or stalkerlike.)

5. If you know anything about a customer's hobbies, interests, pets, kids, spouse, partner, family members, etc., spend a moment checking in about them.

6. Show gratitude to the customer for being a longtime (or first-time) customer, for choosing your company, for allowing you to work on their account, and so forth.

7. Use what I call "spark words," little phrases that ring in a customer's ear with reassurance that this matters to you: both their issue and the pleasure of conversing with them. Here are four such phrases:

   - "Nice [or "Great"] to hear from you [again]!"
   - "I'm your person to take care of this for you from here on out."
   - "If you ever need anything, here's my direct extension."
   - "Now that you have me working on your issue, I'm going to get you the absolute best resolution possible."

8. To make sure customers who are on your premises never feel unrecognized, use the **10–5–3** sequence:

   - When a customer is **10 feet away** (this assumes that they're walking toward you or you toward them), acknowledge their presence with a nod and direct eye contact.
   - At **five feet**, smile.
   - At **three feet**, say "hello," or "good morning," or "good afternoon," assuming the customer is not otherwise engaged (e.g., on their cell phone or talking to a companion with whom they're shopping). If they are thus engaged, *leave them alone!*

Human-Delivered Recognition Is a Slam Dunk. Automated Recognition? Useful, but of Limited Power

An entirely automated acknowledgment trick (a website greeting such as, "Welcome back, [customer name]!") isn't the same as recognition provided by an actual human. Automated acknowledgments do have some impact, but the impact isn't as strong as actual employee-delivered recognition.

To get more oomph out of a technological assist, take the approach with which I began this chapter: use technology *in the background* to prompt the recognition of your own Mrs. Golds. Let technology facilitate, but your humans deliver, the recognition that customers crave.

"Sorry to Intrude, but Can I Get Some Customer Service over Here?"

Customers hate when they're made to feel like an interruption, that feeling that they're not welcome to talk with an employee *they see right in front of them* until that employee wraps up a conversation with their teammate; likewise when an employee who answers their phone call is clearly not focused on them.

You could call this providing *anti-recognition*, I suppose, and it can undercut other efforts to build a positive relationship with customers.

There aren't many companies out there that will flat-out and indefinitely ignore a customer standing right in front of them. Eventually (perhaps very eventually), every customer will receive service, or some semblance thereof.

But does that service happen *after* the nearest employee puts down their cell phone with a tiny accompanying grimace? *After* an employee finishes the file note they're writing? *After* the employee finishes laughing with a coworker about the lopsided score in Sunday's game?

Or does service commence *right away*, with direct eye contact (if the exchange is in person) and a smile (whether on the phone or in person), as if the customer's presence is actually appreciated?

The difference here may be only a matter of seconds, or milliseconds. But what happens within that brief time span can make all the difference in how a customer feels treated by your company.

Your entire workforce needs to be trained to avoid making a customer feel even briefly ignored because an employee is finishing up a conversation with a coworker, or shuffling through papers from a preceding project, or putting the final touches on an email.

Yes, there are exceptions. If interrupting your work could lead to dire consequences, say, if you are a pharmacist in the middle of counting out medication, then please put safety first. But barring that, the masterful approach is to use your peripheral vision, hearing, Spidey-sense, even, to be aware that a customer is approaching. And then stop what you're doing a few seconds *before* the customer makes visual contact. Cut off that conversation you're having with your colleague abruptly, mid-sentence, even; you and your coworker can finish it up later! This way you're fully ready for the customer when they're ready for you.

Here's one tricky scenario and how to handle it without making anyone feel like an interruption or otherwise neglected: What if you're a salesclerk on the phone with a customer, taking their order, when another customer walks up to the counter, ready to pay for their merchandise? In this scenario, it's generally best to politely ask (yes, *ask*, don't demand!) the customer on the phone to hold on for a moment, then tell the person who has just walked up that you're taking care of a customer on the phone and that you'll serve them as soon as you finish up. *The principle is that the person in front of you needs to be acknowledged, not ignored, even if you can't fully serve them in that moment.* (Sometimes, you can actually accomplish this with an apologetic look and a hand gesture rather than making anyone hold at all.)

Providing Your Customers (Particularly Your "Power Users") with Recognition and Simultaneously Letting Them Enhance Your Customer Support

One phenomenon that has grown is the desire of customers to involve themselves with their favorite companies in ways that go well beyond passively making purchases.

You can build on this phenomenon while simultaneously getting some essential help in your customer support if you give recognition to the customers who are already supporting your brand and make active use of their contributions.

When you sell a complex product or service, in particular, the best support you can offer to customers may be
what can be derived from *other* customers ("users") who
are already volunteering their experiences and expertise
online. If you want to consider taking this route, here are
three guiding principles I've gleaned from discussions with
Rani Mani, director for customer success, social media strategy, and engagement at Adobe, the prominent graphics
software company best known for its Photoshop product:

1. **Curate before you create.** "At Adobe," says Mani,
   "our best practice is to assume that when a 'new'
   customer question is voiced, it has likely been asked
   before." This is why Adobe invests a lot in "curation
   time," making sure that, rather than endlessly
   re-creating the wheel, they find the best (the
   roundest??) previously created wheel, i.e., the answer
   that is not just correct but also *most complete*,
   and flag that answer for use when similar queries
   come up.

2. **Reward your "power answerers."** The most
   important source of content here is the assistance
   Adobe gets from the most expert slice of their
   user base, typically referred to as "power users,"
   or, I suppose, they could best be described for our
   purposes as "power answerers." Adobe embraces
   these user experts, giving them perks like free
   Creative Cloud subscriptions and an official badge
   that is of actual professional value. This badge
   identifies the user as an Adobe Community Expert,
   a title the user can add to their marketing materials,
   LinkedIn profile, business cards, and so forth.

3. **When a pain point is pointed out to you by a power user, fix it at the source.** This may mean making a change in the software's functionality, or it may mean adding some introductory panels to the software along the lines of, "Greetings, first-time InDesign user! We recommend you take these four steps before you do anything else; otherwise, you may later be tearing out your hair."

THE POWER OF RECOGNITION
Put the Mrs. Gold Principle to Work

Nearly every customer has a desire to be recognized, to be seen as a unique individual. If you can fulfill this desire, you create a powerful, unspoken reason for them to continue to do business with your company well into the future.

Welcome Back!
One of the best ways to make customers feel valued is to show that you remember them. Keep track of and make use of your knowledge of your customers' hobbies, pets, likes, dislikes, and more, so that even employees who haven't worked with them before know how to form common ground with them.

Focus!
Customers should never feel like an interruption. Employees need to immediately drop any nonemergency activity and give customers their full attention the moment the customer becomes aware of the employee.

Every Customer Is at the Center of Their Own World

Every customer is at the center of their own world. Lean into this reality by making it feel like they're at the center of *your* world as well.

Here are seven simple ways to show your customer they are at the center of your world:

1. Use your customer's name.
2. Tell them your name.
3. If they ask how you're doing, be sure to reciprocate by asking how *they're* doing, too.
4. If you can, say positive or knowledgeable things about their hobbies or other personal passions, or even the neighborhood where they live if it's right there on their shipping form or invoice. (Careful on this last point with celebrities and affluent customers, who may find it intrusive.)
5. Tell them how grateful you are that they are your customer, whether it's their first or hundredth time using your services.
6. Use "spark words" that will assure them they are in great hands:

   - "It's great to hear from you!"
   - "I'm your person to resolve this from here on out."
   - "If you ever need anything, here's my direct extension."
   - "Now that you have me working on your issue, I'm going to fix this right up for you."

(continued)

7. For customers who are in your physical space, follow the
10–5–3 sequence:

- When a customer is 10 feet away, make eye contact.
- When they are five feet away, smile.
- When they are three feet away, greet them unless
they are otherwise engaged (e.g, they're talking to
someone on the phone).

CHAPTER 5

SERVICE RECOVERY

*How to Repair Broken Customer
Relationships and Make Them Stronger
Than They Ever Were Before*

Things do go wrong—sometimes dramatically so—at every business, no matter how wonderfully conceived and manifested it may be. There will inevitably be events, circumstances, and misunderstandings that will frustrate, upset, irritate, disappoint, or even infuriate your customers.

The particularities of these situations can't be predicted in advance. *But your framework for response can.*

Every Great Organization Has a Framework for Service Recovery

Every customer-focused organization has a framework for service recovery that it turns to when they need to turn around unhappy customers.

For example:

▶ The Marriott service recovery framework spells L-E-A-R-N (*Listen, Empathize, Apologize, React, Notify*); the triple-five-star Broadmoor hotel has a framework that (more or less) spells H-E-A-R-T (*Hear, Empathize, Apologize, Respond, Take* action and follow up); and Starbucks has a framework that spells out L-A-T-T-E (*Listen, Acknowledge, Thank, Take* action, *Explain*—how adorable and on-brand is that?).

Meet MAMA

And—you guessed it—I have my own service recovery system and accompanying mnemonic. The framework for which I've become known spells out M-A-M-A, with my promise being: if you learn the MAMA framework and practice it in advance, the next time you're confronted with an upset customer, you'll no longer feel like falling on the floor in a fetal position and crying out, "Mama [or Papa], come rescue me!"

Here in brief, are the steps involved in the MAMA service recovery method. We'll dig into each of these in a moment.

M **M**ake time to listen.

A **A**cknowledge and, if it's called for, apologize.

M Have a **M**eeting of minds.

A **A**ct! and follow up. (I snuck in that "follow up" because I felt that MAMAF would be a less-than-attractive acronym.)

Let's go through these step-by-step, letter-by-letter, starting with the first M.

A CAUTIONARY NOTE: This service recovery approach is not intended to guide you if confronted by an individual who is armed and/or threatening violence.

Handling that is a different discipline, typically referred to as de-escalation training, which is not within my range of expertise. It's not covered here and may diverge in significant ways.

M Make Time to Listen

Immediately stop whatever you're doing. Don't exacerbate the situation by making an already upset customer feel unheard, as if their upset state means less to you than whatever else you may be working on or finishing up. (There are exceptions: certain tasks that are hazardous to stop in the middle, like my prior example of the pharmacist counting out pills. But those are the exceptions.)

Listen with your ears, your eyes, and your body. The positioning of your body can do a lot to convey whether you're listening; *literally* leaning in as you listen can do wonders.

Don't interrupt the customer with questions or explanations. And, very important:

Don't try to solve anything yet.

Don't do it! Instead, listen, listen, listen.

Listening quietly, not interrupting, and not trying to solve things yet is a tough one for most of us, because we want to be helpful and responsive. So, when a customer starts to explain how and why they're upset—managing to get just a few details out about what is bothering them—we tend jump ahead to figure out and suggest a solution.

But, please:

Don't

Don't

Don't

Don't

blurt out your solution yet!

Instead *listen, keep listening,* and then *listen some more.* Let the customer spell out for you what *they* feel went wrong in gory, gory detail. This will provide the customer with a feeling of release and reveal nuances about what transpired that may be different from what you assume is the problem.

Acknowledge and, If Called for, Apologize

Now, acknowledge how unfortunate the situation is. Also, if called for—meaning that *the customer* appears to feel that it's called for, not necessarily that *you* do—apologize.

Even if you have zero reason to feel that you or your company is at fault, or even if you know for certain that you aren't, you should—with most customers—convey to them that you recognize and regret what happened.

"With *most* customers?" Why the hedging, Micah?

Because every customer is different. Some customers are strictly business, either because that's their nature or because that's their role in the situation. For example, they may be transacting with you on behalf of their boss and this issue is not really *their* problem in any emotion-generating way; it's just a problem that needs to get resolved in the course of doing their job. And some customers are simply in a hurry and don't want to be slowed down in any way, including by listening to your apology.

So, what can you do about these variations? Read your customers' cues as best you can and adjust accordingly. I do, however, encourage you to err on the side of being *more* rather than *less* apologetic until a customer's preference for being treated otherwise becomes clear.

If you decide to apologize, make it a good, meaningful apology. Here are three legitimate apologies with substance to them:

> "I'm sorry that this happened."

> "I'm sorry for the misunderstanding."

> "I'm sorry that we let you down."

Although only one of these apologies (the third one) says that you or your company did anything wrong, any one of these three will successfully convey that you're sorry about what's occurred.

By contrast, here are some attempts at apologizing that are so meaningless and insincere that they're probably worse than saying nothing at all:

"I'm sorry that you feel that way." (Yikes.)

"I'm sorry *if* you feel that way." (Double yikes.)

"I'm sorry, I had other jobs that took priority."

Oh boy. This last statement may be true, but, say it with me:

It's . . .

not . . .

an . . .

apology.

M (Have a) Meeting of Minds

Now, strive to align yourself with your customer on what a solution should look like. This step is when you determine what the customer wants in terms of an optimal resolution. Then, if you can't 100 percent agree to what the customer is asking for, do your best to align their request with what would be practical for you to actually make happen, in light of limitations like time and budget.

Include your customer in this process and remain open to an entirely different vision of a solution emerging that's different from what you expected them to be looking for and/or how you've resolved similar challenges in the past.

Once you have a match, *spell out* the agreed-upon solution as you understand it, to make sure you've got it right.

Most importantly, commit to two things:

▸ *What* you're going to do
▸ *By when* you're going to do it

 ## Act! And Follow Up

All that's left is the final step. Or, as I confessed a few pages back, it's more like *two* steps.

First, the "act" part. Take care of the issue as you've promised. Do so by or before the agreed-upon date and time. As you do so, remember that it's often *how* you do something as much as (or almost as much as) *what* you do that will impress a customer with your caring and commitment. Work with your customer in the most gracious, understanding, and patient manner manageable.

Now, the follow-up. There are three types of follow-ups called for:

▸ **Follow up internally with any colleagues involved** (i.e., anyone to whom you've assigned all or part of the resolution. For example, you may have handed off a portion of what you've promised the customer to a more technically inclined colleague. There are two reasons that this internal follow-up is important:

- Something may have gotten lost in translation when you handed off the task (to colleague, by and large, though this could also be a trusted vendor). They may have an erroneous view of the situation's details, since they haven't been in direct contact with your customer. (Think of the game Operator or Telephone and how the initial message inevitably gets mangled.)

- As in sports, any time you attempt to have a ball change hands, the ball is in danger of being dropped.

▶ **Follow up with your customer.** Because it was *you* who made time to listen, *you* who had a meeting of minds, *you* who ultimately made the promises, it can feel unresolved to the customer if you don't follow up with them personally. Moreover, you'll best determine whether you've actually succeeded with the resolution by checking in with your customer.

▶ **Follow up within your company systems in the interest of future improvement.** For the benefit of your entire organization moving forward, someone(s) should examine and log every situation that has required service resolution. This should be done with an eye toward identifying negative patterns and issues such as resource allocation or systems limitations that may be holding you down (short staffing on Thursdays, for example). This way, your organization can patch up what's causing these failures at the root.

Enjoy a free training from Micah on service recovery at micahsolomon.com/training [link is case-sensitive].

* * *

The aim of service recovery isn't exactly to fix whatever went wrong, though of course that is part of it. Your ultimate goal is to *replace the story the customer is telling themself about you, your company, and even about how their day is going with a new, more positive narrative.*

This means that whatever you're doing logistically or financially for the customer can never be the whole point.

The success or failure of service recovery doesn't depend only on the black-and-white specifics of the ultimate resolution. It also depends on the nuances of how you carry this out and the patience and understanding with which you provide service to your customer in this stressful situation. These finer points can do as much as anything to improve the feeling the customer takes home with them.

So, do everything you can to minimize the misery involved for your customer while making things right. In fact, *let the pleasantness of dealing with you on service recovery be part of the reward.* Service recovery can be done in a grudging way, an argumentative way; it can be delivered through clenched teeth. But going about it that way is never going to change the story for the customer, at least not in a positive way.

The Number One Question I Get from Strangers: "Is the Customer Always Right?"

When someone meets me, say on a plane or at the grocery store, and learns what I do for a living, they sometimes get a mischievous look in their eyes. Then they'll spring one particular question at me, as if they've been saving it up for just this occasion, a random encounter with a customer service professional:

"Is it true that the customer is always right?"

And I always take the bait, giving them the best answer I can:

"No, the customer's not always right. But by and large you want to make them feel like they are."

What do I mean by this? A couple things:

- **There is rarely value in correcting a customer when they're wrong,** especially if they're mad as a hornet. Instead, stick scrupulously to your customer service resolution framework. And if you don't have a customer service recovery system in place, yet, remember this: you should always start with listening, rather than with a rebuttal.

- **If you *do* need to correct a customer, don't lead with your correction.** Remember: The customer believes that they are actually right, regardless of the facts. So, start by showing you understand where the customer is coming from; and only *after* that, if needed, you can, like the cops in a thousand TV shows, ask them to "walk me through that one more time."

If the facts do show that your customer is objectively in the wrong, this still may not matter (see the first bullet point above), so you may want to let them continue to be wrong without correction. If you do need to set them straight, help them slowly and gently to come around to this reality. You don't gain points by aggressively or haughtily pointing out the error of their ways.

There Are Exceptions

Here are some situations where you *will* need to let a customer know that they're wrong—immediately and firmly:

- **Safety and security.** If failure to correct a customer's actions or belief has safety or security implications (e.g., "It's not a problem if I move my chair in front of the emergency exit, right?" or "It's no biggie if I prop open the gate on the hotel swimming pool, right?" or "It's okay to leave my baby in the car for 'just a minute' while you check me in, yes?"), then by all means let the customer know the error of their ways right away!
- **Overservice of alcohol.** I wish I didn't even need to mention this exception to making the customer feel

they're "right," but from what I've seen, it still needs to be said.

- **Complex contracts.** Particularly in B2B contexts, contracts and their scopes can go far beyond what the concept of "letting the customer be right" can address. But a "keeping the customer *feeling* right" attitude can still help: when a request (or demand) is made by someone at the other end of a contract, you're more likely to get them where they need to be—and where you can afford to be—without ruffled feathers.

- **Healthcare (the patient experience).** Part of my work is as a patient experience consultant, helping hospitals and healthcare systems improve how they serve their patients and thereby increase patient satisfaction. Success here depends on treating patients like customers in *some* aspects of their healthcare experience, but in other aspects it's important to keep in mind that a patient will never be *exactly* analogous to a customer. Patients deserve gracious service, but they also deserve your gentle but firm "no" at those times when failing to be candid with a patient could affect their current comfort or future health.

If you're aiming to change the feeling, change the story, you shouldn't automatically aim to revert the situation to the way it would have been had the error never occurred. Putting things back the way they should have been, as if the issue never occurred, can be a fine resolution on trivial issues, say,

"My office supply order was short one pen." If that's the complaint, then, absolutely, just replace the pen. (Maybe throw in an extra one if you like, you big spender, you!)

But with any issue that has significantly inconvenienced a customer, putting things back the way they should have been means that *the customer still loses out,* because they've had to go through a whole rigmarole just to get their problem resolved. So, it's ideal if you can both resolve the issue and give the customer something extra for their troubles.

This something extra doesn't always have to cost a penny (though, certainly, sometimes it does). Consider the no-cost extra I received for my inconvenience from an extraordinary employee at FedEx: I had attempted to send a package internationally, but it got stuck somewhere in the system and was overlooked for some two or three weeks until it was ultimately located and delivered through the efforts of this employee, working out of FedEx's headquarters in Memphis. At the end of our multiple conversations, and after it was clear that her intervention had succeed, she asked,

"Is there anything else I can do for you, Mr. Solomon?"

Jokingly, I asked if, since she's based in Memphis, she could stop by the landmark Peabody hotel and take a photo or video of the hotel's iconic ducks on parade in the lobby.

Sure as can be, an adorable video of parading ducks appeared on my cell phone a few days later, to the delight of my kids (and the kid in me). It was enough to *almost* make me want to have FedEx misplace my next package. Almost.

The Service Recovery Paradox— a Scientific Reason to Keep Your Chin Up

When a customer is saying—or even shouting—their dissatisfaction with your company, your coworkers, or even yourself, it can be hard to believe that you could *ever* make that customer happy again and change the story that has taken root in their mind.

But take heart from the *service recovery paradox*.

The service recovery paradox is the scientific finding that a customer's feelings about your company after encountering a problem with your company and then having it resolved to their satisfaction are likely to improve *beyond* how they felt about you before the whole thing erupted. Their post-resolution satisfaction—not always, but more often than not—will be greater than if the issue had never cropped up in the first place.*

You read that right. A well-treated, formerly upset customer is *more likely* to become a fan of, and even advocate for, your business than if nothing had ever gone wrong.

Huh? Why on earth would this be? Perhaps it's because you've now proven yourself to be more than a mere fair-weather friend; on the contrary, your company is now viewed as an ally that can be relied on in bad times as well as good. It also may be, to some extent, because you and the customer have now been through a shared event together and have emerged on the other side unscathed.

---

* The strength of this phenomenon is stronger in some scenarios than others. It appears to vary in strength based on the seriousness of the defect, among other factors. So, I wouldn't recommend trusting the principle to the extent that you're tempted to *introduce* defects in order to then recover from them. Don't worry; plenty of issues will come up organically without any assistance!

Whatever the reason, can I stop for a moment and just say, "wow!"? The service recovery paradox is such a heartening concept to keep in mind the next time a customer is blowing their fuse, claiming, "I'll never do business with your company again!" The odds are good that they'll not only come back around, but will come around with an *increased* level of trust in your organization, so long as you masterfully handle the service recovery.

SERVICE RECOVERY

How to Repair Broken Customer Relationships and Make Them Stronger Than They Ever Were Before

---

S ometimes things are going to go wrong. In the end, though, customer service problems aren't necessarily disasters, thanks to the service recovery paradox, the scientific finding that:

A customer's feelings about your company after encountering a problem with your company and then having it resolved to their satisfaction are likely to actually improve beyond how they felt about you before the whole thing erupted.

You Need a Framework

In order to turn give yourself the best chance of pulling this off, you need a framework for service recovery. Introducing Micah's MAMA framework:

Step 1: M Make Time to Listen

1 Immediately stop what you're doing.
2. Give the customer your complete attention.
3. Don't interrupt with questions or explanations.
4. Don't try to solve anything, yet.

Step 2: A Acknowledge and, If Called for, Apologize

Let the customer know that you regret what happened—even if you know you are not at fault!

If an apology is called for, meaning you sense that the customer wants an apology, not necessarily that you feel it's called for, make that apology meaningful. Don't make an insincere apology or one that puts the blame on the customer!

For example:

Rather than, "I'm sorry if you feel that way,"

say, "I'm sorry that this happened."

Step 3: M Have a Meeting of Minds

Align yourself with your customer and their desires. You may be able to do exactly what they request, or you may need to modify it based on your realities of doing business. Include the customer in this solution-finding process and remain open to a completely different solution emerging from what you'd imagined initially.

Once you have agreed on a solution, be sure to spell it out to make sure you have it right. Commit to two things:

- *What* you're going to do for them
- By *when* you're going to do it

Step 4: A Act! and Follow Up

Take care of the issue as promised, and do so in the most gracious, understanding, and patient manner.

Then, follow up, in three different ways:

- Follow up internally with colleagues: make sure any coworker involved in fulfilling the solution has succeeded as you expected them to.

(continued)

- Follow up with the customer: make sure you have resolved the issue as they expected you to.
- Follow up within your company systems: Every failure that has required service recovery needs to be documented. This allows the discovery of patterns of failure so that your organization can patch up what's causing these failures at the root.

Service recovery isn't just about fixing the problem. It's about improving the story your customer tells themself. Strive to change the story they take home.

* * *

Free resource for readers: **View Micah's eLearning training module on service recovery at micahsolomon.com/training [link is case-sensitive].**

CHAPTER 6

LANGUAGE

The Driver (and Destroyer) of Exceptional Customer Service

Pretty much the first thing I do when kicking off a customer service transformation initiative is determine my client's *current state*: where the company stands, *right now*, in the quality of its customer service experience.* One thing this involves is a short period of mystery shopping, which is carried out by my team and me, on location.

Case in point: I was beginning a project for a client not long ago, a generally high-performing regional bank.† What I encountered at the first branch I visited (incognito) made it clear that the bank's approach to interacting with customers, including the language used in those interactions, was ripe for improvement.

---

* If you want to explore what it would look like to have us work on customer service transformation for your company, email **consult@micahsolomon.com** or visit **micahsolomon.com**.

† Just a reminder that, as with other client examples in this book, the details here have been changed for the protection and privacy of the business in question.

Micah: I'd like to get this document notarized, if you have a minute.

Bank Branch Manager: *I'll need to stop you right there.* Are you a customer?

Micah: Not yet—we're new to the neighborhood.

Manager: That's why I asked. We can only provide notary services for customers.

Micah: Seems like providing notary services could help you *attract* customers, yes?

Manager: Maybe you have a point, but I beg to differ.

Micah: Well, you know better than me. But I am curious—why *can't* you help non-customers?

Manager: It's bank policy. And someone from our central office could stop by at any time to enforce it.

Painful though this exchange was (and still is, reading it back), it was a stroke of good fortune that I experienced it personally and was able to draw attention to the incident in my report to the bank's leadership team. Otherwise, I'm afraid they wouldn't have ever known that any of this had gone down, that such alienating language was being used with prospective bank customers.

Consider how much was at stake in this encounter—and how much is at stake in similar interactions at your own company. A lot rides on whether your employees make appropriate word choices and phrasing. And when they don't? It's a *big problem.*

Language selection is far from a trivial matter. The language that employees use with customers can strengthen (or undermine) a company's ability to successfully connect with—and not fatally turn off—its customers and would-be customers.

Avoid the temptation to think of the subject of language as *just* words. Rather, we're talking about something essential to customer service mastery. *Without the right language, everyone who works with customers is putting the brand they represent at a disadvantage.*

Build a "Say This, Not That" Company Phrasebook

Fortunately, there are systematic ways to improve the language used in your organization.

I suggest you begin by building a phrasebook that identifies the words and phrases that are likely to set a customer's teeth on edge, and pairs these with the alternatives that are most likely to connect with customers and set them at ease.

In this way, it becomes a "Say This, Not That" resource that will keep your whole company, quite literally, on the same page.

The Triple A Language Screening Tool: Avoid • Assure • Align

In considering the phrases and words that should go into your company phrasebook, start by running them through the Triple A—**A**void, **A**ssure, **A**lign—language screening tool. Any questionable phrase—any word or phrase that sounds a little off in conversation with customers—is a candidate to put through this screening.

Avoid • Assure • Align

Avoid
Does the phrase or word *avoid* these pitfalls? Watch out for any words or phrases that would make a customer

> *bristle,*
>
> or
>
> *feel undermined,*
>
> or
>
> *feel like you're spoiling for a fight,*
>
> or
>
> *feel like they are being judged or looked down upon,*
>
> or
>
> *question your company's trustworthiness.*

Assure
Does the word or phrase build *assurance*? The language used with customers should:

- ▸ Build comfort
- ▸ Let a customer know you have their back
- ▸ Reinforce the idea that you have things under control

Align
Does the word or phrase *align* with a service style that works for your brand? Your words and phrases should fit within a

service style that is appropriate to (and, ideally, a pleasant and unique aspect of) your particular brand.

Here Are a Few Phrases That Should Fail If You Use the Triple A Screening Tool

"Let Me Stop You Right There"

This little gem, which was wielded at me in my encounter above with the bank manager, fails as far as the first A in Triple A—to *avoid*. It made me bristle and feel undermined.

It fails as well in a second screening category. As a bonus negative, so to speak, it doesn't fit the goals of the second A, *assure*. It neither built my comfort nor made me feel that the branch manager had my back.

"I'm Not Going to Argue with You"

If you fling this phrase at a customer when a conversation starts to heat up, you're using a phrase that fails to *avoid* a key negative (spoiling for a fight), because you're literally *bringing up* the concept of argument!

"Like I Said," "Again," "Per My Previous Email," "If You Refer to Our Prior Conversation," and So Forth

These are phrases that I sometimes call "concentration shaming." You're pointing out to the customer that they've overlooked, forgotten, or failed to understand instructions or information that you've already provided. For this reason, these phrases fail to *assure*: they do the opposite of making a customer feel that you're there to provide a backstop of support.

Instead of concentration shaming your customer, take a breath and repeat what you've previously said or typed—perhaps using different, easier-to-follow language the second time around.

"To Be Honest with You," "To Be Perfectly Transparent," or "Full Disclosure"

Nobody means anything negative (or, really, anything at all!) when they preface their words with one of these disclaimers. Still, I'd propose that these phrases fail to *avoid* seeming untrustworthy and fail to *align* with an optimal service style. (What is a customer supposed to imagine you were doing *before* you became all honest and transparent? Lying through your teeth?!)

*   *   *

More on the subject of alignment: There are also words and phrases that won't align with a brand's style for either lack of formality or excessive formality: *"No worries," "You bet," "Gotcha,"* and so forth on the one hand, and *"Sir," "Ma'am," "At Your Service,"* and the like on the other. Some businesses benefit from sounding informal, while others are at their best when they sound more reserved and straightlaced. Also, keep in mind that B2B companies are generally safe using jargon and abbreviations with their customers (at least if those customers are in the same or a related industry), while most B2C businesses should avoid these like the plague.

More Language Dos and Don'ts

Here are half a dozen additional language guidelines that will keep you on a good footing with your customers.

The *"No Problem"* Problem

If a customer thanks you, what should you say in response? Let's imagine an auto repair shop where a customer at the service counter graciously says, "Thanks, Jim [the service advisor], I appreciate the time you put into explaining what was wrong with my engine."

Here's one possible response. Let's say that Jim responds with, *"No problem."*

How does Jim's response strike you? To my ear, there are multiple things wrong with Jim's response.

The first one is that "no problem" brings the idea of a problem to the forefront. That little "no" in "no problem" isn't enough to outweigh the more vivid concept of "problem," which Jim has unintentionally brought up.

It's hard—perhaps impossible—to succeed in convincing someone to *not* think about something. (If you want to test what I'm saying, try right now to *not* think about a delicious ice cream sundae.)

The other thing wrong is that "no problem" downplays, rather than honors, the time and consideration that the customer put into giving thanks. If a customer goes out of their way to convey their gratitude, you'd do well to acknowledge it.

Here are better ways to acknowledge a thankful customer and even return their thanks:

"You're welcome."

"Thank *you*!"

"It was my pleasure."

As a side note, "No problem" is a perfectly fine and appropriate way to minimize the discomfort a customer feels after they inconvenience you or do something embarrassing. "I'm sorry I spilled my soda on your carpet" or "I'm sorry I clogged the toilet in my guestroom" is, in fact, better replied to with "It was no problem" than with something hoity toity like, "It was my pleasure [to clean up your soda or plunge your toilet]".

The Money Language Pit

Money—particularly money owed—is a subject that, if talked about too directly, can be off-putting to customers. I'd avoid telling a customer something like,

> *"Hey Pat, you still owe us $339,000,000.33."*

Pat may indeed owe you that money, but this phrasing makes you sound accusatory. It's like you're saying that Pat wants to drag his feet or even abscond without paying down his $339-million-and-change balance.

The same point could be better conveyed by,

> *"Our records show a current balance of $339,000,000.33."*

Same point, gentler language.

The "How Are You Doing?" Ping-Pong Game, and the Importance of Not Letting the Ping-Pong Ball Drop

When you're responding to a customer who's just asked,

> *"How are you?"*

I suggest you reply with,

> *"I'm doing great. How are YOU?"*

Any response along these lines is fine. The important thing is that you *reciprocate*—returning the verbal ping-pong ball to the customer's side of the table—rather than letting the "how are you?" ball drop to the floor.

Admittedly, the "how are you?" ritual is a basically an empty exchange. But since it's the *customer* who has initiated it, it's important that you support your side of an important part of communication: reciprocity. So, please don't just reply with,

> *"Good,"*
>
> or
>
> *"I'm fine,"*
>
> or
>
> *"I'm well,"*

and let the conversation die right there.

Likewise, please do not answer with a chilly,

> *"I'm well; how can I help?,"*

without first asking the customer how *they* are doing. Your offer of assistance does not replace the need to provide reciprocation to their inquiry into your wellbeing. In fact, it arguably makes the implication that such pleasantries are a waste of your time and that the customer should hurry up and get to the meat of the conversation.

Humor in Customer Service

As a customer, I enjoy humor. I can still make myself chuckle by thinking back to the time I asked for coffee on JetBlue and the flight attendant replied,

> *"Give me a minute to burn a new pot for you."*

Or, when I was on a Virgin America (now a part of Alaska Airlines) flight, and the pilot came out of the cockpit to apologize for the late departure and promised to

> *"fly it like we stole it," and still get us to our destination on time.*

And on Southwest, when the flight attendant warned passengers who prematurely unbuckled their seatbelts rather than waiting for the chime,

> *"I'd keep your seatbelt on if I were you. He's a great pilot, but he's a lousy driver."*

There's also the bartender I heard promise to rescue someone at the bar

> *"from the throes of sobriety."*

And the waitress who, when I mentioned the bountiful serving size said,

> *"I apologize. Is it too much food for the money?"*

Or the dentist who, when I doubted his claim that I was grinding my teeth at night, told me,

"Well, somebody has been."

And the time I told a woman answering the phone at a new vendor that I found their prices surprisingly reasonable and she shot back,

"I can raise them just for you!"

The upside to injecting your personal brand of humor into customer service is that it can be memorable, disarming, and an instant bonding experience. The downside is that it's hard to know your audience and predict their sensibilities and sensitivities.

For me, the "burn a new pot" implied that "we're all in this airplane cabin experience together, and I'm going to help you enjoy it by using my whole personality." But a less understanding (grumpier!) passenger might be inspired to tweet, "The coffee standards are so low on this airline that even the flight attendant realizes it."

In a nutshell, the challenge is that you're guessing when it comes to humor—and guessing is always risky. So unlike most other hard-and-fast language guidelines I can lay down for you, this is an area where it's better if I just leave it at "use your best judgment." Good luck, buttercup!

Avoiding Defensive Language

Defensive language is language you use to push back against anything you perceive as an attack. Which is exactly the wrong way to respond to a customer. Defensiveness makes you sound like you're gearing up for a fight, but, by definition, you can never win a fight with a customer. Never! If you "win" (and I use those quotation marks advisedly), your company loses! It's as simple as that.

So, if defensive responses are so counterproductive, why do we use them? My theory is that this goes back to how we interacted as children with our siblings—or, if we didn't have a sibling, with our peer group at school.

Let's say my brother tried to get me to stop riding our new scooter so that he could have a turn, saying (with exaggeration, no doubt), "Micah, get off now and let me have a turn—you've been on it *all day.*"

A Training Video from Micah on Language in Customer Service, Including "The Problem With No Problem"

A Resource For Readers: For a free video training segment on the "no problem" problem and other language do's and dont's: visit micah.pub/noproblem [link is case-sensitive].

So, reflexively, I snap back with defensive language (and, no doubt, an exaggeration of my own): "I have not. I just got on it. It's *you* who always hogs the scooter, not me!"

If such counterattacks had any value when we were kids, the same approach can have catastrophic results now that we're adults.

Especially when we're interacting with customers.

Avoid These Defensive Phrases

Here are some defensive phrases to avoid at every turn:

"Really?"

"Well, you shouldn't have done that!"

"You should have done [such and such]."

"Nobody working here would ever have done that."

"That's not how we operate."

"That's not our fault."

"I've worked with her for years and I've never seen her do anything like what you describe."

"That's not our responsibility."

"That's not true."

"That's incorrect.

"That couldn't possibly be what happened."

Getting these instinctive responses out of your approach can take practice. It's not all that easy to avoid blurting one of these out when a customer is in your face or on the phone line, accusing your company, and possibly you, of dastardly deeds. But it's essential.

Alternatives to Defensive Language: Neutral Expressions That Don't Put Anyone on the Spot

Here are some neutral expressions that avoid accusation and even encourage collaboration:

> **"Do I hear you** [that you expected such and such]?"

> **"If I have this correct,** [you feel that Angela told you your order would arrive, rather than merely being shipped, on March 1]."

> **"It sounds like** we really failed to convey [_____]."

"Perhaps" and **"alternatively"** are also great words to use when it's time to start suggesting different theories of what went down:

> **"Perhaps** [Angela intended to convey that . . .]."

> **"Alternatively,** [Reggie may have thought you'd be dropping off your keys Monday through Thursday, not on a Friday just before the weekend shutdown]."

If a Customer Says Something Incorrect, Avoid Correcting Them (By and Large)

If a customer says something incorrect and the error *doesn't matter* (let's say they misquote a sports score or they're convinced that John and Paul wrote "Taxman," when you *know* it was actually George*), don't contradict them, don't correct them, don't say anything to advise them that they're wrong.

And if a customer makes a mistake or exhibits a misunderstanding that you *do* need to point out (perhaps their mistake or misunderstanding has safety implications or needs to be corrected so they don't keep *repeating* the mistake in the future), make it seem like a mistake that *anybody* could have easily made.

Here's an example of a mistake in this second category, one that you might want to (gently) point out, for the good of the customer.

Working in a repair shop, you put a customer's car up on the lift and discover a pattern of wear in the rotors and brake pads that indicates the customer has been habitually riding the brakes. If you're going to tell them something potentially embarrassing like this (which I'm not entirely sure I would), I'd suggest handling it like this:

> *Riding the brakes is hard on a car, but it's an easy habit to get into, and it's actually one that implies you're safety conscious. Believe me, I know this personally. For the first five years after I started driving, my foot was on the brake almost all the time. It was only when I started working here and saw the wear and tear on some of the cars up on the lift that I realized what was going on.*

Do you see my point? If you *have to* draw a customer's attention to an error they've made, frame it as an easy-to-make, common error, even if the reality is that this is the first time that anyone has ever walked into your world and made it!

---

* Duh!

Words Without Words

Some of the language that can rub a customer wrong is what I call "words without words":

- **Appearing visibly displeased.** This can be shown by your expression, posture, or lack of eye contact.
- **Giving negative auditory cues.** This includes sighing, shuffling papers, typing loudly, and so on. I confess that I've been guilty of this last one; I've been told I sound like I'm mad at my keyboard when I'm typing. (Not good, Micah, if there's danger of being overheard by a customer!)
- **Failing to match a customer's pacing.** This is when a customer is unhurried and leisurely, but you seem impatient, like you're trying to hurry them out of your presence or off of the telephone. Or, the other way around: Your customer is in a hurry, but you're dragging things out. (This can happen when you're busy trying to put some gold-touch—"tell extra"—into a conversation [you're really Micah-ing them!], but if you were paying attention, you'd pick up on their cues indicating that they want to get off the phone or out the door.)

  - **Not being ready when a customer is ready to be served.** If a customer is in front of you ready to be served, or if they've called in and you've picked up the phone, the situation is now cut-and-dried: you should be ready to talk with them rather than taking care of, or remaining preoccupied with, something else.
  - **Not yielding at a potential collision point.** When a customer is sharing a physical environment with

you, your awareness can go a long way. This includes yielding to customers rather than barging ahead of—or even *into*—them when you reach a potential physical collision point.

If a customer's walking through, say, your company's showroom or waiting area, on a beeline toward one of the exit doors, and you're walking at a right angle to their path (maybe you're en route to refilling the copier paper), your route is going to eventually intersect with theirs. This leaves you three options:

Option 1: The Worst Possible Approach

You're so distracted thinking about, say, your kid's lousy report card—or your kid's phenomenal report card, for that matter—that you practically run over the customer. You never yield, never modify your route. Instead, the customer is made to yield.

Option 2: A Tolerable Approach, but Still Not Anticipatory

This time, your head is only *halfway* in the clouds, so you do, eventually, become aware of the customer, but only at the *last* minute. And at that last minute, you say, "after you," and yield to the customer.

While this is a whole lot better than nearly running the customer over and forcing them to yield, it still fails to *anticipate* an entirely predictable event. And by failing to apply anticipatory thinking, you're creating a moment of tension for a customer who will be interrupted and set on edge by the interaction.

Option 3: Applying Anticipation to the Upcoming Intersection

By keeping your eyes open and paying attention, you recognize *early on* that a potential collision is looming. You pause or adjust your path so the customer can proceed on their way without a near miss and without ever needing to know that there was the potential for collision.

* * *

Free resourse for readers: For language dos and don'ts in a handy, printable reference format, send an email to words@ micahsolomon.com. Please also introduce yourself and tell me a bit about yourself and your business situation in your email!

LANGUAGE

The Driver (and Destroyer)
of Exceptional Customer Service

The words and phrases that are used in interactions with customers can drive—or undermine—your organization's ability to successfully connect with them. If employees who interact with customers aren't using the right language, they put your brand at a disadvantage.

Create a "Say This, Not That" Company Phrasebook

Create a simple book for your organization that spells out which phrases to use and which ones to avoid.

Not sure which words to include? Use my Triple A checklist: Avoid, Assure, Align.

> **Avoid** words that will anger the customer, challenge them, make them feel undermined, or question your company's trustworthiness.

> **Assure** your customer with words that build comfort. Let the customer know you have their back and have things under control.

> **Align** your language to make sure it fits with your brand. Language that may work for one company will not work for another. For example, the language used by a five-star hotel should differ from the language used by a store

(continued)

that sells nutritional supplements, particularly in level of formality.

Avoid Defensive Language

Such as:

- "We would never do that."
- "Are you sure that's what happened?"
- "Well, you shouldn't have done that!"

Instead, use neutral expressions that don't sound like you're picking a fight, such as:

- "If I have this correct . . ."
- "It sounds like . . ."
- "Perhaps, . . ."
- "Alternatively, . . ."

Other phrases to avoid:

- "I'm not going to argue with you." This has the opposite effect of what you're intending.
- "Like I said," "Again," or "Per my previous email." Here, you are talking down to and shaming the customer for not paying attention or comprehending to the level you'd expect.
- "To be honest with you" and "Full disclosure." These phrases make it sound like you haven't been up-front with the customer thus far.

- If a customer thanks you, avoid saying, "no problem" in response. It downplays the consideration that the customer put into thanking you.
- If a customer asks how you are, reciprocate with "I'm great. How are *you*?"or a similar phrase brings the attention back to them.

Other Tips to Put Your Customers at Ease

- Be aware of your body language. You can say all the right things, but if you appear to be annoyed or displeased, the customer will notice.
- Match the customer's pace: don't make them think you are impatient to get the interaction over with; conversely, if they seem in a hurry or to be "all business," strive to match that faster tempo.
- Be aware of where your customers are when they're on the move within your physical environment, so you never make them need to yield to you at a potential collision point.

CHAPTER 7

TECHNOLOGY

*Harnessing Its Power Without
Losing the Human Touch*

"I'm more scared of this than I am of *bears*!" the CEO of a retail business in the Midwest confessed after I gently suggested she increase her reliance on technology to serve her company's ever-growing customer base.

Her bigger-than-bear-sized terror,* as my client explained it to me, was that technology would take a bite (sorry) out of the friendly, hands-on customer service that her company, founded by her grandfather some 50 years ago, was known for, as personable, human-delivered service had played a big part in the company's growth to prominence within the craft and hobby space.

---

* She's actually an avid Northwoods hiker, where bears are far from an abstraction.

"We're known for being hands-on people," she explained. "It's how we stay so close to our customers. We hire good people, we train them well—as you know—and we do everything we can to keep them inspired. And, so far, it's working."

The numbers bear* this out: sales in most categories increase year-over-year, customer reviews are positive, and employee satisfaction is through the roof.

Of course, I understand her skittishness and the protectiveness she has for her existing (and very successful) way of doing business. Her company's human-on-human approach is a large part of why her customers are so fiercely loyal; she'll get no argument from me there.

What I *did* point out, however, is that in today's commercial landscape, even her most loyal customers are going to grow frustrated if the tools her company uses to serve them don't evolve with the times.

Why? Because, as time inexorably marches forward, the comparison to more tech-enabled competitors will make her company's response times feel laggy. The lack of instant answers via self-service (including outside of business hours) will grate, and a multitude of other customer inconveniences (*relative* inconveniences, based on what the competition has put into place) will steadily drive an ever-larger wedge between her brand and its customers.

Plus, there are so many positives my client could reap for customers (and for her employees) by incorporating the wonders of technology into her approach. These could include:

▸ Using AI-enhanced tools to keep frontline staff apprised, in nearly real time, of any price changes,

---

* I'll stop now.

delivery restrictions, or late-breaking developments that could affect a phone call, email, or text exchange. This would both empower the employee and provide greater convenience and accuracy to the customer.

▶ Expanding channels and improving ease of contact for existing customers and new prospects alike, without ever losing track of anything that's been typed out (or even *thumbed* in a text) at any point in the customer journey.

▶ Offering customers the option to check the accuracy of account and project information 24-7.

▶ For homebound crafters, making use of 360-degree views and/or augmented reality to allow them to dive more deeply into the products available at her stores, without leaving their living room. Crafters could use this technology to immerse themselves, in depth, into her company's offerings of frames, thread, adhesives, and more.*

▶ Using automated transcription of recorded calls to review and improve the quality of customer interactions.

▶ Harnessing the power of data to offer cross-selling and upselling that will actually be *welcomed* by the customer, because such suggestions are more likely to be relevant rather than intrusive. Far from a

---

* Likewise, in other industries, car dealers can use augmented reality to let an interested buyer "into" a minivan's third row to see how it would feel back there with kids, without requiring an initial trek to the showroom. Hotels can show people around their chosen rooms. Landscaping companies can show how a potential improvement would look on a customer's actual lot. And realtors can transform the process of purchasing a home via the view that such technology can provide into nooks and crannies—as well as using virtual staging to place furniture, paintings, and other décor where there isn't any.

clichéd upsell like "Would you like fries with that?," AI-powered assistance can provide recommendations that are well tailored to a specific situation. In the case of my client and her crafting customer base, it can suggest, for example, picture frames that are appropriate for a particular aesthetic, or an adhesive that will lift cleanly from a particular type of surface.

The Importance of Aiming for Digital Parity in Every Line of Business

Nearly every business would do well to strive for digital parity. *Digital parity*, as I define it, is the idea that:

> *Every business, no matter how brick-and-mortar it may be, should be as good on the technology side of how it interacts with customers as fully digital, entirely e-commerce players are.*

It's hard to think of a more archetypal brick-and-mortar institution than Ace Hardware,* with its more than 5,000 physical locations—a number that is growing, despite ruthless, predatory attacks from big-box stores and massive online competition. Ace makes great use of its physicality, including by hosting in-store (more precisely, in-parking-lot) events like its pre-holiday Thanksgrilling get-together, where expert employees, who have been trained at Ace Hardware's internal BBQ Bootcamp, share grilling tips and related know-how.

---

* You can even buy bricks and the makings of mortar at their brick-and-mortar stores!

Yet Ace Hardware recognizes that no matter how tactile and pleasing the experience of visiting a physical store or attending an in-person event may be, the only way to fully serve today's customers is to couple the in-person experience with up-to-snuff online and mobile experiences.

In fact, *more than 90 percent of Ace customers perform the initial research phase of their shopping online.** Ace has responded apace, building its site into one of the top search engines for the items it sells, from hardware to snow shovels to outdoor sheds to birding supplies. Likewise, once Ace determined the extent to which online tutorials are favored by its customers, it began to augment on-location events with brief "tips and tricks" videos and full-length instructional videos.

Part of the Ace Hardware advantage has always been that the in-store experience benefits from the involvement of a hardware professional—sometimes the actual store owner—greeting an incoming customer with a series of questions that facilitate a successfully personalized shopping experience. Now, customers who start their visit to Ace online can experience similar personalization via an intelligent process that guides the user through a series of questions until useful, personalized results are achieved.

Delivery is another place where Ace has been merging the in-store, online, and mobile experiences, pursuing what is often called an "omnichannel strategy," an approach that has grown in popularity among retailers. Customers can order online and pick up at their local Ace store. Or, the experience can flow in the opposite direction, with customers ordering

---

* Judy Mottl, "Ace Hardware Goes Thanksgrilling in Customer Service Strategy," RetailCustomerExperience.com.

in-store for home delivery rather than needing to schlep home whatever they've purchased.

Importantly, all purchases regardless of channel are logged on the Ace Hardware website and app, allowing for easy repurchase. And a customer's purchases or ideas for future purchases can easily be shared with friends or colleagues.*

Finally, Ace uses technology to improve its localization, ensuring that each store offers the precise product mix that customers in its local market are likely to desire. This offers a strong advantage in competing against big-box stores, even with their massive store footprints. By using up-to-the-minute inventory reporting and proprietary AI that can predict upcoming buying trends, Ace has increased its ability to keep items in stock that its local customers hope to find.

Keep Your Technology Below Eye Level

If you want to use technology to bolster your customer service while keeping it from interfering with the human relationships you have with your customers, here's a concept to keep in mind:

Strive to keep technology below eye level.

For a *literal* example of this concept, think of how all technology is kept strictly below the customer's line of sight at the registration counter in an upscale hotel. This arrangement allows hotel employees to maintain eye contact with arriving guests, who never need to be aware of the technological

---

* "Ace Hardware on the Importance of Seamless Omnichannel," PYMNTS.com (March 16, 2020).

backbone informing employee responses. The result appears to be, and in a sense *is*, magic, at least in the hands of well-trained, personable front desk employees. That's because the terminal with all the good stuff—individual guest preferences, quoted rate, housekeeping status of every room, and the like—is kept below, and completely out of view of, the customer.

How Below-Eye-Level Technology Keeps Last Night's Room Service Detritus Out of View at This Triple-Five-Star Hotel

Isn't it nasty to stumble over a room service cart or tray covered with soggy reminders of someone's (perhaps your) late-night food choices, now looking worse for the wear in your hotel's hallway?

As a hotel guest himself, this has long been a pet peeve of Daniel Hostettler, president of The Boca Raton, a multiple five-star resort in Southern Florida, and the former president of Ocean House, likewise a multiple five-star* seaside resort in Watch Hill, Rhode Island. In response, he devised his own technological solution to keep the corridors free of all such room service memories: "I embedded microchips in the room service carts, and put a chip reader in the guest room doorframe, so that when a guest pushes the cart into the hallway, it sends out an alarm to our staff." This is not

---

* Only a small number of hotels achieve a *single* five-star rating from *Forbes*, and far fewer achieve multiple simultaneous five-star ratings. Triple five stars, for example, means five stars achieved in each of a property's three key offerings: lodging, food, and spa.

just a single-beep alarm, by the way, but one that keeps ringing loudly and flashes until an employee acknowledges the alarm and collects the cart.

Hostettler says this is an example of one of the passions that drives him as a hotelier, "using technology behind the scenes, that the guest never sees, to deliver a five-star customer experience." And that, I have to say, is a pretty good definition of the principle of below eye level technology.

In other business scenarios, the principle of keeping technology below eye level won't be applied quite so literally, but it's a valuable conceptual model, nonetheless. Even if some technology *does* need to be visible to the customer,* for example at an insurance company that equips its claims adjusters with tablets so they can work carside in the customer's driveway, proper employee training can keep this technology from excessively interfering with the customer experience. Such training and sensitivity are called for because you want, *at all costs*, to avoid becoming one of those companies that gives employees tablets with clunky software and insufficient training, resulting in more employee energy and attention spent interacting with the tablet than with the customer in front of them.

* * *

---

* Self-service is inherently an exception to the below-eye-level model, but don't use this as a reason to look disparagingly at self-service's popularity with customers: there are going to be situations where your customers will want to work with self-service technology directly—times when, if your self-service is well designed and thoughtfully deployed, all you'll need to do is get out of the way.

Digital Anticipation

Here's an additional concept to guide your deployment of technology: embrace technology's ability to power anticipatory customer service, to provide what I call *digital anticipation*.

Up to this point, the picture I've given you of anticipatory customer service probably makes it seem entirely employee-driven, as if it were powered *solely* by empathetic employees with their antennas out and ears perked up. But even if that's the customer's impression (i.e., the exterior view) of an anticipatory customer service encounter, the use of technology to back up those employees can allow them to bring more to a customer encounter than just their native instinct and awareness.

Consider Sweetwater Sound, a billion dollar musical instrument dealer offering everything from electric guitars and keyboards to the brass instruments, woodwinds, and drums that power both school and armed services marching bands.

Primarily an online and catalog business, Sweetwater serves musicians remotely from its 100-acre, 320,000-square-foot facility in Fort Wayne, Indiana. Sweetwater is serious about making sure that the product choices it offers are selected and arranged sensibly to make sure a customer can find what they're looking for without delay or detour. To accomplish this, Sweetwater makes use of deep staff knowledge (they have an employee base that's nearly 95 percent musicians, recording studio owners, video professionals, and the like), while bolstering that staff knowledge with the latest in anticipatory AI and algorithmically driven technology.

The power of this marriage between humans and advanced technology can be illustrated with an app-based or website search. A customer—in this case, let's assume a keyboard player—might use the Sweetwater website search field to look for "sustain pedals," the pedal that sustains a note or chord on a keyboard after it's played. Although this search bar is informed by AI and does its best to winnow out invalid results, a customer who performs this search is confronted with, as I count them, more than 80 options. Some are obviously relevant, some clearly not, and some fall in a grey area. At this point, a human being—a fellow keyboard player, ideally, on Sweetwater's staff—becomes the best choice to help sift through these daunting inventory results for the pedal that would best suit the customer's specific keyboard setup.

The Triangular Model of AI and Similar Advanced Technology in Customer Service

Let me give you one more model that I find helpful: the triangular model of tech-enabled and human-powered customer service. This triangle helps to visualize the multiple ways customers and employees may interact with and benefit from AI and similar high technology, as well as interacting, at times, directly with one another.

The Three Vertices in the Technology– Customer–Employee Triangle

- ▸ **Vertex 1:** The *agent*, or other human service provider. (In the Sweetwater example, an employee working the phones or corresponding by email or chat with the customer.)

▶ **Vertex 2:** The *customer* or prospect.
▶ **Vertex 3:** *Artificial intelligence* or other high technology.

customer

agent

ai

or similar technology

The triangular model of AI in customer service

© 2024 Four Aces Inc., Micah Solomon, President

In the triangular model, the information exchange at the heart of customer service can come . . .

. . . via self-service, with AI or another high-tech tool serving the customer directly without any involvement from customer service professionals. This initial customer engagement with intelligent technology can sometimes answer a customer's questions completely, right off the bat. In this case, only two vertices of the triangle are engaged: the customer and the technology they're using. Not only that, but *actions* that the customer is trying to achieve can sometimes be triggered without any human involvement. For example, AI-informed technology can generate a return authorization or even issue a refund to resolve a minor issue—say, $5 for being a day late in delivery. (This is what's going on at Amazon when you try to return something very trivial and a decision is made on the fly to credit you *without even making you return the item*, based on a) your record as a good customer on prior transactions and b) the item being too inconsequential to be worth the hassle of receiving it back into inventory.)

From a human employee who, in turn, is likely aided behind the scenes by AI and similar technology. (Here, all three vertices—customer, employee, and technology—are engaged, but the third vertex, technology, is invisible to the customer.)

From a combination of these two forms of support, with the customer switching from one to the other as they see fit. The customer can *start* with self-service, such as an AI-powered search bar on the company website (which, by the way, is a solution that is superior to the traditional, always out-of-date FAQ approach), then *switch* to working with a human employee if needed, when the time comes. In other words, if the self-service tools are no longer giving your customer or prospect what they're looking for, a human agent can then intervene—either at the request of your customer (clicking on a "Click here for . . .") or at the discretion of the company.

Note that, per the *interactional* nature of our triangle, *even after* the customer begins interacting directly with a human, advanced technology will still likely be helping out:

▸ **On the agent side,** AI can prompt the employee with pop-up messages onscreen that offer context-based suggestions for how to best serve the customer. These in-the-moment prompts can be so powerful, in fact, that they can *enable generalist employees to handle specialized inquiries* and challenges that they wouldn't have been able to before.

▸ **On the customer side,** there's no reason to assume that your customers will stop using technology on their own the moment they're interacting with a human employee. Rather, most will continue poking around on the company website or searching for an answer via the world's largest receptacle of anticipatory results, Google.

TECHNOLOGY

*Harnessing Its Power Without
Losing the Human Touch*

Technology, when used properly, can be a boon for customer service:

- It can speed up response times, offering instant answers to customers.
- It can keep employees updated on price, delivery, and other frequently changing data points in near real time.
- It can enable customers to check on their account or project on a self-service basis 24-7.
- Via online or app-based features (like 360-degree views and augmented reality), it can provide customers with information and context on a prospective purchase or similar.
- The use of AI can identify the ideal cross-selling and upsells for a particular customer—offers that will generally be welcomed, because they are likely to be relevant to that particular customer.

But you have to be careful not to lose the human touch. Strive to keep technology *below eye level*, where it can assist staff but does not get in the way of the human relationships you're building with your customers.

The Importance of Aiming for Digital Parity

Every business, no matter how brick-and-mortar it may be, should strive to be as good at the technology side of how it interacts with customers as the fully digital, entirely e-commerce players are.

The triangular model of AI in customer service.

© 2024 Four Aces Inc., Micah Solomon, President

The Triangular Model

The triangular model of tech-enabled and human-powered customer service illustrates the multiple ways customers and employees may interact with (and benefit from) AI and similar technology.

(continued)

The three vertices of the triangle are:

- The *human service provider* (the company employee) at the first vertex of the triangle.
- The *customer or prospect* at the second vertex.
- *Artificial intelligence or other high technology* at the third vertex.

All three of these vertices can be involved in customer service via a variety of pathways.

CHAPTER 8

COMMUNICATING VIA TELEPHONE

How to Use the Least-Sexy Customer Service Channel to Keep Your Cash Registers Ringing

alking on the telephone is a pretty unflashy form of communication. Yet the telephone's ability to provide human-on-human interaction with real-time cues continues to make it a powerful brand builder. In today's varied, tech-informed customer support landscape, the venerable telephone conversation stands out more than ever before. That's because:

- With the rise of digital communication and self-service, telephone conversations between customers and brands have become *rarer*, and thus *more precious*. When a customer only interacts with you on the phone once or twice in their entire journey with your company (rather than every day or even multiple times a day), every call represents a chance to make a real and lasting connection. This single interaction can go on to create a halo of personal connection and care that can positively color all those other electronic, often non-peopled interactions that are so typical today.

▶ Customers are typically *in greater need* when they do reach out to a business on the phone today. They're more likely to be at their wit's end, dealing with a thorny problem that self-service tools have failed to answer. In this situation, they're likely to feel gratitude for every ounce of phone skills you can command.

A Telephone Conversation Is Your Chance to Shine

A telephone conversation offers multiple clues as to what is going on emotionally on both sides of the conversation, including tone and volume of voice, speed of speech, length of pauses, and more. This affords you the ability to adjust your approach immediately in response, which can improve your ability to solve problems with empathy and to deepen your customer connections.

This, in turn, can help you shine as a brand and as an organization and help you make strides toward becoming legendary for your customer service.

To start out on the right telephonic foot (so to speak), a business should consider the answers to the following questions:

▸ *Who* **should be answering our telephones?** Someone fabulous! Unfortunately, though, it's common for companies to consider reception and phone support to be entry-level jobs—positions that an employee is supposed to graduate from as quickly as possible. But isn't it safer to put entry-level employees in positions that are *hidden* from customers, rather than front and center, where they become, literally, the voice of the company?

In my experience, the right employee to become the voice of your company is someone who *isn't* looking to graduate quickly from that position, but is instead willing to devote themselves to making the most of it. And be sure you don't count out those of an advanced age! In my experience, a grandparent, parent, or someone else with extensive and varied life experience is often the person who can provide a calming, empathetic, personable phone experience better than anyone.

▸ *How quickly* **should we be picking up?** It's best to pick up at or just after the third ring. By the fourth ring, callers start to feel uncomfortable, doubting whether you'll *ever* in fact pick up, and begin to assume that if you finally do, you'll be too distracted, overwhelmed, or flustered to be much help.

Many of the highest-touch brands, such as Nordstrom and the Ritz-Carlton Hotel Company, have taken the 3-ring rule to heart. (In fact, it's a standard of the *Forbes* Travel Guide rating system; you get points taken off if you let your phones ring four or more times.)

▶ *What should we say* **when we answer?** The best way to answer a ringing phone is with a greeting that includes all four of the following elements (this is easier than it sounds, as you'll see when we get to the examples):

1. A greeting
2. A business identification
3. A self-identification
4. An offer of assistance

Example 1:

Good morning, **(The greeting.)**

Business [X]. **(The business identification.)**

This is [Jerry]. **(Identifying yourself.)**

How may I help you? **(Your offer of assistance.)**

Example 2:

Thank you for calling, **(The greeting.)**

Business [X]. **(The business identification.)**

This is [Jerry Smith]. **(Identifying yourself.)**

How may I help you? **(The offer of assistance.)**

Example 3:

"Welcome to [business], **(Combined greeting *and* business identification.)**

This is [Jerry]. **(Identifying yourself.)**

How may I assist you? **(The offer of assistance.)**

Don't Make Your Greeting Too Wordy, Even If a Branding "Expert" Tells You To

It's smart to keep each of the four elements brief. I would advise against trying to jam in branding elements beyond identifying your company;* otherwise, your greeting will grow so long that employees will have no choice but to rush through it. We've all experienced those fast-casual restaurants whose telephone scripts have metastasized, à la the following:

> *Welcome to TGIMondays, home of the weekly special on ultra-spicy wings and our new online ordering—we'll bring them to your car before you can say "Monday." This is Melanie, would you like to order our weekly special today?*

"The Call Is Coming from Inside the Building": How to Answer *Internal* Phone Calls

For internal calls, it's fine to answer more briefly and with less formality, using only two of these four elements. One of these two elements, however, should always be your name.

Internal Example 1:
Good morning. This is [Jerry]. **(Using two elements: greeting and self-identification.)**

Internal Example 2:
[Department Name,] [Jerry] speaking. **(Using two elements: business identification and self-identification.)**

---

* Though there have been some charming exceptions to this advice, like Umpqua Bank gutsily answering their phones with, "Welcome to the world's greatest bank!"

Internal Example 3:
[Jerry Smith] here—how may I help you? **(Using two elements: self-identification and offer of assistance.)**

What Should You Sound Like When You Pick Up?

Fabulous, of course! Achieving this will depend on multiple elements working in concert:

- ▶ **Make sure you're smiling.** When you smile, it changes your vocal tone in a way that is easy to pick up, even within the limited audio range of a phone line. Some veteran phone professionals even use tape or Velcro to stick a compact mirror at eye level in their workspace to remind them to smile every time they pick up the phone. (I know this is dorky, but it works.)

    A caution about sounding cheery and smiley at the wrong time: Once you've given your initial greeting on the phone, it becomes time to start *emulating* the mood of your customer. This will sometimes call for something other than a cheery tone of voice. Once you know the nature of the customer's call and their mood, you can drop your smile if indicated. (If the customer is explaining how she fell down the stairs yesterday and broke both legs, you don't want to sound all chipper and smiley: "Oh! [smile smile]; I'm so sorry to hear that!")

- ▶ **Make sure that you sound focused on the caller from the very first second (millisecond, even) that they hear your voice.** Customers can sense even the briefest moment of disengagement at the beginning of a call.

Pause any prior activity before answering the phone to be sure your mind is focused on the call—and that you sound that way.

▶ **Pay attention to audio quality.** Those of you who are in, or preside over, a shared office: Do whatever you can to avoid the boiler room effect that comes when other voices can be overheard by the caller. Noise reduction technology is only of limited use here, as technology is best at reducing noise when you're *not* talking, which means the noise can come flooding back whenever you do speak. So, an already quiet environment is the best place to start.

Also, with the popularity of working from home, the variety of systems and handsets (or lack of handsets) being used has grown. It's worth the investment to make sure that every employee, in every environment, is using a system that is up to snuff.

▶ **Avoid call screening if possible; if not possible, go about your screening gently.** Customers and prospects rightly take umbrage at being run through a series of intrusive questions about why they are contacting you and the nature of their call. If you must use screening questions, imply that the callers *will* get through regardless of who they are. Make it seem that the info you're requesting is for professional purposes, rather than to screen for who does and doesn't get past the velvet rope.

For example, for a caller who's asked to speak to Ms. White, instead of grilling them with, "May I ask who's calling?" say, "Absolutely—may I let Ms. White know who is calling?" Using this more encouraging wording makes a world of difference.

A widespread problem I encounter is how many employees in the labor pool have been mis-trained by a previous employer and come to work at a new job armed with a routine along the lines of:

"Your name?"

"Uh huh. And what company do you represent?"

"Okay, and what is the nature of your call?"

This is customer- and prospect-repellent behavior. It's important to *train it out of* anyone who has been mistrained in this manner, in part because it's contagious—you'll soon hear other employees mimicking this intrusive line of questioning themselves.

More Tips for Starting off a Phone Conversation

▶ **Immediately show that *you value the caller's name* if they share it with you.** This is an easy and effective way to make use of the power of recognition:

"Hi, this is Juanita Johnson."

calls for a response of,

"Hello, Juanita!"

or,

"Good morning, Ms. Johnson!"

Or, even better, if she's a repeat caller,

"Great to hear from you [again], Juanita!"

or

"Great to hear from you [again], Ms. Johnson!"

The point here is to avoid the scenario where a customer offers their name and then is made to feel awkward or dumb for having done so. In other words, *avoid*:

Customer: "Hi, this is Michele Hernandez."

Employee: "Yes?" (Yikes!), or,
"Okay, How can I help?" (Again, yikes!)

Either of these responses, by failing to acknowledge that the caller has offered their name, is bound to make them feel that, when they went out on a limb by offering their name, you left them out there on that limb to dangle!

▶ **Remember to not overuse the customer's name as the conversation proceeds.** Make use of your customer's name *within reason*. I'd caution you against exaggerating the frequency with which you use a customer's name beyond what would be natural in everyday speech. Otherwise, you'll end up sounding like a clichéd, wide-lapeled salesperson, artificially filling in every blank in the conversation with the customer's name.

Guidelines for Transferring a Call

▶ **If your phone system allows, make sure that the intended recipient of your transfer picks up before you disconnect.** If nobody picks up, return to the caller and offer alternatives for what to do next.

▶ **Don't automatically let an attempted transfer go to voicemail unless the caller requests this or has provided permission to do so.** Many callers are leery of voicemail, believing (reasonably) that few employees check their voicemail regularly. If you encounter this resistance, provide other options, such as offering to take down and convey the message personally.

▶ **Before making a transfer, inform the caller that you're about to do so.** *("Judy, please allow me to transfer your call to . . .".)*

▶ **Strive to relay the caller's information and the nature of their call (if they've shared these with you) to the recipient of the transfer.** *("I have Dwayne Richardson on the line, and he's been having a technical problem related to his online subscription. This is his second call.")*

▶ **It's likewise useful to restate shared information when you're the *recipient* of a transferred call.** *("Hello, Jerry [or, "Hello, Mr. Smith"], my colleague Joanne tells me that you're calling about your prescription. I'm here to help you with that.")* This spares the caller from repeating themselves and allows them to correct you if you have incorrect information about the nature of their call.

Placing a Caller on Hold

▶ **Obtain permission: "Would you mind if I place you on a brief hold?"** This is important. Even though nearly every caller will agree to hold if you ask them to, they still want to know that they have a choice. Think of a parent calling a pediatrician's office. Ninety-nine times in a row they're probably fine with holding, but they want to make that choice *for themselves* every one of those times. This allows them to feel reassured that if, on the 100th time they call and they *can't* hold—their kid is having seizures, let's say—they have the option to demand immediate attention.

▶ **When it takes some time to process a caller's request, come back on the line with the caller.** Thank them for holding and ask if they'd prefer to continue holding or would like to be called back.

> **Note:** For those of you whose customers are often forced to wait in a queue, consider installing a callback system. This allows a customer to speak with you at a specified time of their choice, rather than making them wait on the line . . . no matter how scintillating you think your hold music is!

End Every Call with a Fond Farewell

Ending your call on a good note—providing a "fond farewell"—is as important (or nearly as important) as getting the opening of your call right. This is because of the *proximity effect*, the psychological finding that the very last part of an interaction tends to linger in memory.

As the call is winding down, ask if anything else is needed. If the caller answers "no," conclude the interaction with a personal farewell that includes their name and perhaps another detail like, "It's been great working with you, Margaret. I'll see you back here on Thursday and I'll call you if anything changes." Also, if it's appropriate to the situation, invite them to call on you for assistance in the future.

Effective Phrases to Personalize Your Farewells

"It was great working with you, [Margaret]."

"It was great meeting with you."

"It was nice spending this time with you today. See you next time!"

"Have a good drive home."

"Enjoy the sunset."

"Have a great rest of your day; I'll be in touch by Thursday—or earlier, if there's any news."

Other Telephone Principles

▶ **Conform to the pace of the caller as soon as you decipher it, reducing or increasing how fast you speak depending on the cues you're picking up.** Some callers are in a huge rush; others are as leisurely as the day is long. And to make this trickier, *the same customer* might be slow-paced and chill on their first call in the morning, but as tightly wound as the inside of a golf ball when they call you back later in the day.

▶ **When you answer the phone, *you own the call.*** In other words, by picking up the phone, you've taken the responsibility for successfully getting the caller to the next step in their journey. This may involve personally handling the caller's request, or it may mean successfully transferring them to a more appropriate person. Remember that callers *hate* being bounced around and made to repeat their requests or to re-share information they've already provided. So, the more informed you can make the next point of contact, the better.

▶ **"Have the last word" every time—that is, a comment in response to whatever the customer has just voiced, rather than letting what they say dangle in dead air.** This sophisticated telephone technique is more easily illustrated than explained.

Caller: How are you?

Employee (having the last word, in this case, in a follow-up response): I'm doing great, how are you?

Caller: Great, thanks for asking. Would you please connect me with Mrs. Smith?

Employee (having the last word): I'll be happy to transfer you right now.

Caller: Thank you!

Employee (having the last word): You are welcome! Mrs. Smith is on the line, please go ahead.

Caller: Thank you!

Employee (having the last word): You are very welcome!

> **Note:** The "have the last word" technique does slow down a conversation, so you might want to limit its use with a rushed-sounding caller.

▶ **Before using a speakerphone (in a room where there are other people possibly or definitely listening in), ask for the caller's permission.** And avoid using a speakerphone in an open space where the sound would negatively affect your colleagues.

▶ **When making an outbound call to a customer, resist using an autodialer system that doesn't allow you to hear how the person you're calling answers the phone,** which can be off-putting to a customer who answers the phone. For example, if a customer you've called were to pick up the phone and say, "Hello, this is Micah," and then hear you say, "Hi, this is Jane from [X], is Micah there?," it's clear that you haven't heard that I, the customer, have already introduced myself.

▶ **In your voicemail greeting, or when leaving a message in a customer's voicemail, *don't speed up* when sharing your digits or anything else that may be hard to decipher.** Say any numbers or unusual name spellings slowly, and always be sure to repeat them. This repetition will be a godsend to someone who's listening to your message: it allows them to write down these important tidbits without rewinding. (On the other hand, if you're confident your phone number is showing up on their caller ID or via their linked contact list on their cellphone, you don't necessarily need to recite your number at all.)

▶ **There are technical skills involved in using the phone. Everyone should learn and become fluid in those skills, even if they think they'll only be answering the phone once in a while.** A quick example: with your system, does putting the receiver down in the cradle to end a call (rather than hitting the "disconnect" button) cause an unnecessary click or bang? You don't know? Find out!

The Promise and Power of Text Messaging

Now that I've spent much of this chapter selling you on the power of voice-based telephone support, I want to go in another direction: I'm going to encourage you to embrace text messaging between customers and your business.

Messaging allows customers to communicate with companies in a natural way that they're *already* using with their friends, family, and coworkers. In their personal, nonconsumer lives, your customers spend more time texting than they do on voice calls, and this is true across all demographics. Although younger customers do the highest percentage of texting, the difference between even the oldest and youngest thumb-wielding human beings is modest. (And, clearly, a lot of text messages are exchanged *between* generations, such as, "Mom, don't be late to pick me up today, please," or even, "Grandma, can you Venmo me some money so I can treat my friend on their birthday?")

And this preference for texting extends into their lives as customers. Sixty-three percent of people surveyed in the United States report that they would rather message with a brand than call a customer service phone line.* Considering this, it's narrow-minded to continue requiring customers to only contact you by voice.

---

* "When It Comes to Communicating with Businesses, Customers Overwhelmingly Prefer Texting (Infographic)," survey by Avochato. Other surveys show a similar or even stronger preference for message-based service.

The Power of Video Conversations in Customer Service

Support via video conversation is like "voice-and-then-some" support. It offers the auditory cues of a phone call, along with the addition of eye contact and body language cues. As such, video chat sessions tend to engender more empathy on both sides of the call.

Making use of video in creative ways can help an employee and customer consider options and work out solutions together. Think of how useful this can be, for example, when determining fabric and finishes in the home furnishings industry or making color and size choices in apparel retailing. Realtors have become adept at using video calls to allow prospective homebuyers to preview potential homes, to the extent that they can look into drawers and closets "together," without requiring the prospective homebuyer to trudge all over town. Likewise, if a retail store's employee wants to demonstrate the fluffiness of a particular pillow being considered by a customer, a well-placed, on-camera pillow squeeze can speak louder than words.

And here's an interesting phenomenon: the younger the customer, the more their online life is driven by video—and this includes how they prefer to interact with brands. "When you get to Gen Z and younger customers, we're finding their strong preference is for video chat and similar visual tools," says Shannon Flanagan, a retail and e-commerce expert at Talkdesk, a cloud-based contact center and artificial intelligence software provider.

One handy thing about text messaging is that it provides the opportunity for a conversation to be picked up where it left off, even when the customer's on the go. Your customer's initial message could reach you on a Thursday afternoon, when they first discover a problem with their bill. But then, they have to rush to pick up their kids at school, which interrupts* the texting session before everything gets resolved. Their second message might not be sent until the following morning; during that interlude, the agent will likely have been able to research their account history in detail. No rush, and no need to proceed without complete information or fully considered responses on either side of the interaction.

This compares positively with the ideal but oft-abused real-time nature of a phone call. Many businesses require customers to waste their real time (!) getting put on hold or into a queue. Then, once the customer is actually speaking with an employee (perhaps after a long and inconvenient hold time) both the customer and employee are forced to interact *right then*—whether it's actually the best time for either.

In other words, after a customer has finally made it through the queue to talk with an employee, they're only able to speak with that employee for a set period of time. If the customer or the employee disconnects, the customer (who may have one question they've forgotten to ask, or one detail they didn't think to have clarified while the clock was ticking) goes right back into the queue—probably unable to ever talk with that particular agent again to complete the conversation.

---

* I've assumed they're not those evil people who continue to text once they're driving.

Certainly, there are ways to improve this scenario in voice support, such as offering callback times, investing in staffing to shorten the queues, and making sure that agents have as much pertinent data as possible at their fingertips. Still, for some customers—particularly those *already* embittered by the kind of phone (non)support they've received elsewhere—it's attractive to simply do an end-run by allowing those customers to message you at their own convenience. Messaging offers the chance for a conversation to be nearly as real time as a voice call, and allows for a lot more fluidity in how that time is allocated.

COMMUNICATING VIA TELEPHONE

How to Use the Least-Sexy Customer Service Channel to Keep Your Cash Registers Ringing

---

The telephone is one of the most powerful brand builders you have. Why?

- Telephone calls have cues for both participants (tempo, tone of voice, on-the-fly language changes, etc.) that allow both the employee and the customer to adjust as the conversation progresses.
- With so many other support channels now available, telephone calls are relatively rare these days, so every phone call has more impact than it used to.
- These days, if a customer is reaching out by phone, they are likely in greater need, with a thornier-than-usual problem. This allows you to heighten your impact if you handle the call well.

Don't Automatically Assign Telephone Reception to an Entry-Level Employee

You want the most deft and talented employees on the phone. Don't overlook your more senior employees and applicants for these positions!

(continued)

How to Answer the Phone

Be sure to include:

1. A greeting (e.g., "Hello").
2. A business identification (e.g., "Thank you for calling X-Corp").
3. A self-identification (e.g., "This is Patrick").
4. An offer of assistance (e.g., "How may I help you?").

Variations based on these four elements can be found earlier in the chapter.

Internal phone calls can be answered less formally, with a shorter, two-element greeting, as long one of those elements is your name.

How Should You Sound on the Phone?

- Make sure you smile when speaking. People can hear the difference.
- Focus, focus, focus! Customers can tell if you're not paying attention.
- Avoid handling customer service calls in a loud room or with sub-par equipment. Handsets are your friend!

Avoid Unnecessarily Screening Calls

If you do need to screen calls, do it with tact. Use language that suggests the caller's *already* made it through the screening (e.g., "Absolutely! May I let Ms. White know who is calling?").

Placing a Customer on Hold

Make sure you get their permission first. Get back on the line with the customer if it's taking too long to process their request.

Other Telephone Tips

- Make sure you answer *before* the fourth ring. Customers get nervous once a phone rings that fourth time; they worry that you will never answer or that you'll be overwhelmed and distracted if you do eventually pick up.
- Match your customer's pacing.
- Use the customer's name if they give it to you, but don't *overuse* it to the point that it sounds phony.
- Get permission before using a speakerphone (if that speakerphone is in a room where others may hear).
- Use the "have the last word" technique—never let a customer's comment hang in dead air.
- Remember to conclude every call with a fond farewell.

Other Communication Options

- Texting (messaging) is a channel preferred by many consumers and has many advantages for both the customer and the agent.
- Video calls offer even more cues than a voice call. And studies show that younger customers are particularly attracted to video-based support, so it's likely that the value of this channel will increase in the future.

CHAPTER 9

PUT IT IN WRITING

The Secrets of Exceptional Correspondence with Customers

The ideal correspondence to send to your customers is personable, thoughtful, clear, and free of jargon, and—if this is appropriate to your brand—funny, quirky, or otherwise distinctive. If you're hitting most or all of these targets, then your correspondence will have the power to build and sustain relationships and elevate how your organization is perceived.

On the flip side, correspondence that is confusing, incomplete, irrelevant, or insensitive to the nuances of the situation can easily detract from customer relationships.

In spite of the potential power, positive or negative, of correspondence, most businesses haven't even *considered* how they're doing in this area or what they need to improve.

Let me remedy that now, with my ABCs of corresponding with customers.

The ABCs of Corresponding with Customers

Anticipate

Provide anticipatory customer service in your correspondence by including the following:

▶ **Everything your recipient may need.*** This could include information, links, attachments, and the like, whether they've thought to request these or not.

▶ **Answers to questions they may not have thought to ask.** Perhaps the customer doesn't yet understand enough about the situation to think to inquire about a certain topic. For example, if this will be your correspondent's first time in your office and they ask when the building opens, a complete answer might be more than:

"The building opens at 8 a.m."

It should perhaps look more like the following:

"The building opens at 8 a.m.—and security is a stickler about checking IDs. I learned this the hard way my first day here, when I realized I had neglected to bring my driver's license with me."

---

* But don't pile on excessively; including irrelevant information does no favors for anyone.

Beating the Customer to the Punch with Proactive Correspondence

Correspondence doesn't always have to be in response to a query, concern, or, for that matter, an outcry. Get in the habit of proactively reaching out to customers when you have something that would be helpful for them to hear, rather than waiting for them to get in touch with you. (But please don't flood their inboxes and waste their time!)

One airline, in fact, has a proactive customer communications department (isn't that a refreshing concept, compared to the outdated idea of a complaints department?) that does things such as reach out to passengers after a delayed flight with an apology and a modest credit for future travel. They do this even when they have no regulatory obligation to do so, and even when there hasn't (yet) been an outcry from inconvenienced passengers.

Whether or not you're up for actually creating your own proactive customer communications department, the concept is a great one. It's not really that complicated: A fabulous little physician's office in my neighborhood proactively contacts patients when their vaccination status is about to lapse, when health recommendations change, and so forth, simultaneously providing a choice of appointment days and times. In this way, their patients don't need to regularly check their vaccination records, keep up with the latest health advice headlines in the news, or pound the practice's phone lines to ensure an appointment is scheduled.

Anticipation Also Includes Anticipating
What *Doesn't* Matter to the Recipient

▶ Don't include a recipient in an email (directly or cc'd) who doesn't need to read the correspondence.

▶ Avoid routinely hitting "reply all" on every email you receive (unless your company's correspondence retention rules require you to do so). Save "reply all" for when it's truly necessary.

▶ And, it should go without saying (but it needs to be said!), consider whether writing a piece of correspondence is even necessary in the first place, and whether, in its current form, it will be welcomed by your customer.

B Build Your Customers Up; Don't Break Them Down

Written language is a powerful tool. Word choice can make customers feel better or worse about themselves and, by extension, their relationship with your company.

Personalization is a big part of building customers up:

▶ Personalizing how you address them (your salutation)

▶ Customizing the details you include in the body of the correspondence

▶ Personalizing your own name and contact information

This last point is an important one. Close your letter in a friendly way that makes it clear this was a personal letter, as well as providing the customer with easy, *direct* ways to reach back out to you.

Avoid all of the following "worst practices":

▸ Writing an individualized letter to a customer and then signing it generically, "From your friends at _____."

▸ Sending emails from a "donotreply" email address (unless this can't be avoided, which is sometimes the case).

▸ Including only a generic switchboard phone number that requires multiple leaps for the customer to actually reach the person who signed the letter.

Instead, assuming your security principles allow, provide your *actual name* and how to reach you *directly* in the future.

Should You Hand-Write Notes to Customers?

Maybe.

If done well, a handwritten card or letter can be powerful. (In fact, here on my desk, I have a lovely stack of handwritten thank-you notes that I have received myself and continue to treasure.)

But doing it well isn't easy. It means making every note personal rather than one-size-fits-all. It means spelling every word correctly—and you'll need to do this without the aid of autocorrection.

Most of all, it means *actually getting around to it*. Odds are that you won't (at least in my experience); at most companies, well-intentioned initiatives to start writing notes, or even postcards, by hand are abandoned very quickly.

One more negative: *A handwritten, physically mailed note isn't easy for a customer to respond to!* When a customer receives correspondence via email, there are just one or two steps required to reply. Not so with a handwritten note. There's no obvious reply mechanism other than physically mailing something back by what they used to call "return post," which, let's face it, isn't going to happen. This may not seem like a big deal, but if you want to spark (or reignite) an interaction with a customer, you're making that more cumbersome than it might be..

Clarify

One of the reasons we use written correspondence is to have a record when it matters. So, the *clarify* principle is about attention to detail: making sure that what you're putting down in words really is correct information, presented in an understandable way, as if it is truly *for the record*.

Bringing clarity to your correspondence means rereading what you've written to make sure it's both correct and easy to comprehend. If anything you've written could be ambiguous to the recipient (*which* outstanding invoice you're referring to, which entrance you mean, even whether you mean a.m. or p.m., and so forth), use the extra words needed to make your meaning crystal clear (or delete the unnecessary words that obfuscate your meaning). And scan the draft of your correspondence to spot—and get rid of—any internal jargon and abbreviations that would throw off a reader from outside your company or industry.

Ripped from Real Life: A Correspondence Critique and Reworking

Now, let's dig into some actual business correspondence that I recently reworked for a client company, which they're now graciously allowing me to share with you.

A bit of background: The correspondence we'll go over below was sent to me when I was mystery-reviewing the correspondence being sent out by a successful e-commerce company specializing in sports equipment. I did this by using the company's online form to ask which virtual golf package would suit me best, providing a few details of my (imaginary) situation. In response, I received a reply that wasn't *bad*, but could afford to be spiffed up quite a bit. With their permission, here's the original version of their letter:

Original Letter, *Before* My Modifications

Good morning,

Thank you for reaching out. With your available space I believe you would be best suited with one of our [Product X] packages. Below is a link to our most popular [Product X] Package: [a link was inserted here].

Please take a look and let me know if you have any questions.

Best regards,

Customer Support
GenericWebsiteURL.com
(###) ###-#### (generic switchboard phone number)

Now, Here's the Letter After I Modified It, with Indications of My Reasoning Behind the Changes

Dear _____ [*here, we're using the prospective customer's name*],

Thanks so much for reaching out to our team at [company name] for advice on choosing your new golf simulator! [*Thanking them enthusiastically for their interest and making it clear from the get-go that this is going to be a* **custom** *response to a* **specific** *question.*]

Based on the specifications you've given me for your available space, an ideal product for you is most likely the _____. I've put a *link* here where you can check it out.

I'm also available M–F at [phone number] for any additional questions or if you want to look at other options [*encouraging contact and including a **direct way to to respond to whoever signs the letter***]. You can also simply *reply to this email* [*again, encouraging and facilitating a direct response*] and you'll get me or one of my great teammates.

You're going to have a great time with your new simulator, whichever one you end up selecting (and, again, *I'm available to help you with that choice*). It's great to be able to play and practice on world-class golf courses all over the world right from home. And, one of my own favorite features is the option to play against your friends as well! [*Showing enthusiasm and highlighting a special feature.*]

Thanks again for reaching out to us, and I wish you tons of success and lots of enjoyment [*thanking them again and showing shared enthusiasm*],

[Employee name]

PUT IT IN WRITING

The Secrets of Exceptional Correspondence with Customers

The written language is a powerful tool when used correctly. It's best when it's:

- Thoughtful
- Clear
- Jargon-free
- Personable

Your correspondence may also benefit from being funny, quirky, or otherwise distinctive, but only if that's appropriate for your brand.

To further guide you, here are three principles.

The ABCs of Corresponding with Customers

A: Anticipate

Do:
- Give the customer everything they need (info, links, attachments)
- Answer questions they may not have thought to ask, but will benefit from knowing the answer to

Don't:

- Include excessive attachments and links unrelated to the needs of the customer or the issue at hand
- Hit "reply all" unless absolutely called for
- Include people in an email if they don't need to read it
- Send out correspondence that simply wasn't necessary in the first place

B: **Build Your Customers Up, Don't Break Them Down**

Do:

- Personalize how you address the customer (the salutation)
- Customize the details in the body of the correspondence
- Provide your own name and contact info (for an easy reply) in the body or at the end of the letter

Don't:

- Write an individualized letter, but then sign it generically ("From your friends at _____")
- Send emails from a "donotreply" address unless that's unavoidable
- Include only a generic switchboard phone number that will require multiple leaps for the customer to reach you

(continued)

C: Clarify

- Make sure that what you're writing is correct—review it carefully as if it is is truly "for the record."
- Take the time to ensure your meaning isn't ambiguous on any points, such as whether you're referring to a.m. or p.m., the specific invoice you're discussing, and so forth.
- Scan your correspondence one more time to spot any internal jargon that may be meaningless or off-putting to someone outside your company or industry.

Should You Send Handwritten Notes to Customers?

These are sometimes considered the gold standard in personal communication with customers. However:

1. They very rarely actually get written; a well-intentioned initiative to do so quickly falls by the wayside when people get busy.
2. Even though a handwritten note can be lovely to receive, it takes a lot more work for the recipient to reply. So if one of your goals is to get a response from—and spark or continue a dialog with—a customer, a handwritten note isn't the easiest way to accomplish this goal.

—— CHAPTER 10 ——

SURVEYS AND BEYOND

Find Out What Your Customers Really Think (If You Truly Want to Know!)

Surveys, more often than not, are a type of communication that comes out a hot mess.

Sending out poorly designed surveys can:

- ▶ Try the nerves of even your most loyal customers
- ▶ Misguide you with spurious results
- ▶ Waste the time of everyone involved—those who send it out and those who receive it

Designed and deployed properly, however, surveys can reveal essential insights into how customers view their experience with your company—as well as give customers an opportunity to vent!—while treating both respondents and those who choose not to respond with respect.

I encourage you to spend a few minutes with me learning the dos and don'ts of designing and deploying customer surveys.

Twelve Principles for Designing and Deploying Effective Customer Surveys

1. **Every survey question should be clearly worded and easy to answer. It shouldn't require your customer to do math or think too much about the inner workings of your company.** Avoid anything along the lines of, "Compare this interaction with interactions you've had at similar departments at other fintech companies in our broadly competitive cohort." Also: don't ask questions you don't care about and already know you're not going to act on. (This seems obvious, but it happens all the time.)

2. **If you can avoid it (and maybe you can't), don't ask your customers to grade you on a scale of 1–10 or 0–10.** No customer on the planet can determine the difference between a "six" and an "eight" when filling out such a beast. *Provide your customer with a maximum of five choices,* though limiting them to three is even better.

3. **The *order* in which you ask your questions matters, because a prior question brings up images in a customer's mind that will influence their answer to the next one.** So, be sure to ask for your customer's *overall* impression first. You don't want to influence how a customer answers this central question by asking your

more nitpicky questions before you get to the most important, overarching one.

Asking several individual questions before asking for an overall rating will tend to color that overall rating, perhaps quite significantly. For example, if the question the customer encounters *just before* the big one asks about the cleanliness of your restrooms, which was just so-so, this is likely to reduce your overall rating, since you've left their mind in the toilets. Conversely, if they've just been asked about the availability of parking and, in fact, parking was abundant, this is likely to artificially increase your overall rating, since they are thinking about something positive (how easy it was to park).

4. **Include at least one open-ended field (for example, "Please share any thoughts you may have; we promise to read all of these!").** Doing this is valuable both to harvest customer insights and to let customers know you're actually interested in their thoughts and insights.

5. **Word choice matters.** I'm a fan of emotive ratings options on surveys, such as "fantastic!" (for your top score), "meh" (for somewhere in the middle), and even "you don't want to know!" (for your lowest). (Only consider this approach if it conforms with your brand style! It *wouldn't* be appropriate for, say, a traditional jeweler or a business in a life-and-death industry like healthcare or mortuary services.)

6. **Pay attention to the number of top ratings you get back (e.g., a five if the range is one to five or zero to five), especially on your most overarching question.** This is arguably *more important* than your average

score, because the number of people who rate you as tops is the best representation of the number of truly loyal customers you have—or, at least, the number of customers well on their way to true loyalty.

7. **If your survey is lengthy, allow respondents to stop mid-survey and still have their survey count.** This is a lot better than scolding (and invalidating) them for not getting all the way to the end.

8. **Don't ask intrusive demographic questions such as income, gender, or age unless you make such questions optional.** First off, you can never assume that respondents will trust your privacy practices. Second, unless you're a casino operator, cannabis dispenser, or operate another type of business limited by law to serving adults (or if you're in healthcare, banking, or another highly regulated field), you don't have a reason to ask for a complete day-month-year birthdate. If you are trying to set yourself up to later send out birthday cards or offers, please at least stop asking for the *year* of birth. A complete birthdate (a) is probably none of your business and (b) makes identity theft all too easy in the event of a breach.

9. **Skim through your surveys right away, looking for any complaints or ultra-low scores.** Then respond personally and immediately to these upset customers. *Don't make them wait without a response, stewing in their own frustration, until such time as you've batched all your surveys for review.*

10. **Send a personal thank-you note (email is fine) to anyone who gave you a compliment in a free-form field.** Again, do this as promptly as possible.

11. **Put thought and attention into any preamble (cover letter or introductory paragraph[s]) that accompanies your survey.** Your introduction, like the survey itself, should be friendly, gracious, and brand appropriate. This way, whether or not the recipient chooses to respond, they'll be left with a positive impression.

12. **Don't hound your customers if they don't respond to your survey request.** I would make *one* follow-up reminder the limit (or even zero, though I doubt you'll ever go that low). And, once you've surveyed a particular customer, *suppress future surveys of that same customer for at least 30 days.*

* * *

A Customer Survey You Can Borrow from Me Verbatim

Here is a survey I constructed for one of my clients (who is OK with readers emulating or even copying verbatim). I will caution you: *Only you* can determine its applicability for your particular context. I'm certainly not promising this survey is right for everyone!

I've included the opening remarks that precede the survey as well, because starting on the right foot in your introductory remarks is an important part of gaining acceptance from the potential surveyee.*

---

* I was dubious, but "surveyee" appears to be a bona fide word!

We'd love to have your input!

Dear [Firstname],

The [Company Name] customer support team recently had the pleasure of working with you. We hope the feeling was mutual! Either way, we'd love to hear about your experience.

We've made this survey as short as possible to take up very little of your time, but we've also included free-form opportunities for you to vent at length, sing our praises, or share ideas.

And we promise: **we read every one of these.**

Thanks so much,

[Name]
President and CEO
[Company Name]

1. OVERALL, how satisfied were you with your recent experience with [Company Name]'s customer support?

   ☐ Delighted   [3]

   ☐ Reasonably satisfied   [2]

   ☐ Dissatisfied   [1]

   ☐ Not applicable to my situation or I prefer not to answer   [0]

2. What MOST influenced this satisfaction rating?

   ☐ My advisor's knowledge and effectiveness

   ☐ The resolution of my issue

☐ The phone/communication experience (hold times, ease of getting through, availability of email and other channels/options)

☐ Other: _____

_____

3. Was your issue resolved?

☐ Yes

☐ No [Sorry! Please explain below.]

☐ Sort of

_____

_____

☐ Not applicable to my situation or I prefer not to answer

4. How much do you agree or disagree with the following statement as it applies to the most recent [Company Name] employee you spoke with:

"The agent listened to me and showed an interest in my issue and in me."

☐ Agree strongly   [3]

☐ Agree somewhat   [2]

☐ Disagree   [1]

☐ Not applicable to my situation or I prefer not to answer   [0]

5. How much do you agree or disagree with the following statement as it applies to the most recent [Company Name] employee you spoke with:

"The agent was considerate and respectful."

☐ Agree strongly [3]

☐ Agree somewhat [2]

☐ Disagree [1]

☐ Not applicable to my situation or I prefer not to answer [0]

6. How much do you agree or disagree with the following statement as it applies to the most recent [Company Name] employee you spoke with:

"The agent was effective and well informed regarding my issue."

☐ Agree strongly [3]

☐ Agree somewhat [2]

☐ Disagree [1]

☐ Not applicable to my situation or I prefer not to answer [0]

Help us improve: What could we have done better?

_____

_____

Any other advice, comments, praise, or complaints you'd like to share? (Again, I promise that we read every one of these!)

_____

_____

_____

_____

Thank you again for your time, and for being a [Name of Company] customer!

Sincerely,

[First Name of CEO—either use an italicized font or use an actual signature, but note that there may be fraud and identity theft risks if you use an actual signature.]

A Technology-Based Alternative Approach That May (or May Not) Be Better Than Traditional Surveys

Some large consumer-oriented companies, such as American Express, have begun de-emphasizing traditional surveys and started depending instead on technological tools for sentiment capture and analysis. This technology records and transcribes customer calls and then provides a sentiment score for each call.

The theory behind abandoning traditional surveying is that surveys are *transactional* (or, to state that more precisely, they're a response to a particular transaction), and for that reason inherently limited.

If you want to do a test to see whether a technology-driven approach is superior to a traditional survey-based one, here's a way to make that determination:

1. Listen—yes, as human beings, with your ears!—to a certain number of your calls and note your responses to them. How would *you* grade the sentiment you heard?
2. Concurrently capture those calls with technology and let your technology decide what it feels the sentiment score should be.
3. Send out a traditional survey to the customers who were on those calls.
4. Review those survey responses as well as the sentiment-capture approach and determine which result most closely matches your human impression (what you experienced back at Step 1).

According to Amex, their new surveyless approach is much better—90 percent better!—at matching the impression of the humans who listened to the same call, compared to the accuracy of the responses they received from their traditional surveying approach.*

However, even if you have scientific validation such as this, you are left with a paradox. What you have here is a 90 percent better match (at least in Amex's experience) to the impression that *internal listeners* (employees) had of those calls. But is it possible that a survey still, inherently, provides a better match to the *customer's* own impression? There's no clear answer to this—at least, not yet.

---

* Rich Hein, Dom Nicastro, and Michelle Hawley. "CX Decoded" podcast from CMSWire, March 22, 2022, https://www.cmswire.com/podcasts/cx-decoded -by-cmswire-podcast/.

SURVEYS AND BEYOND

Find Out What Your Customers Really Think
(If You Truly Want to Know!)

C ompanies can use surveys to gain useful insight into how customers view their experiences. Here are some of the do's and don'ts of surveying:

1. The best rating scale is one with the fewest choices: one to five, or even one to three. Anything with a range greater than that is too complicated for a customer to weigh in on (what, after all, does a four or a six or a seven represent?)

2. The *order* of your questions matters. Each question will influence the next answer. So, ask for your customers' *overall* impression first.

3. Don't ask questions that require your customer to do math, or to engage too many of their brain cells—no "calculate on a percentage basis how much of your opinion on this is related to . . ."

4. Give the customer the freedom to express themselves by including at least one open-ended question like, "Please share any thoughts you may have."

5. Word choice matters. Consider using emotive words like "dreadful" to "fantastic!" (But only if these conform to your brand style.)

6. Focus on the number of top scores you get (e.g., a five on a scale of one to five). This will give you a sense of how

(continued)

many truly loyal (or on their way to being loyal) customers you have, and whether this number is increasing.

7. If your survey is lengthy, allow respondents to stop midway and still have their survey count.

8. Make intrusive demographic questions (income, gender, age, etc.) optional, or don't ask them at all. Specifically, don't ask for birth *year* unless you're required to by law (or if you're in healthcare, where it's a valid data point).

9. Skim through the results you receive right away and then *immediately* respond to customers who expressed frustrations in your open-ended field(s).

10. Send a personal thank-you email to anyone who gave you a compliment.

11. Carefully craft the survey's introductory language, making it friendly, gracious, and brand appropriate.

12. Don't hound your customers. Send, *at most*, one follow-up reminder to customers who have yet to complete the survey.

13. There are some tech-based alternatives to surveying available; take some time to consider these as well.

CHAPTER 11

CUSTOMER SERVICE EXCELLENCE IS A MOVING TARGET

How to Build a Culture of Innovation So You're Always Keeping Up

Let's stop talking about *your* business for a moment and consider the experiences our customers have every day when they're *not* buying from you—when they shop at other businesses and use public services in their daily lives, as well as any time they use a newly invented or updated product. All of these experiences continue to grow more and more convenient; more and more anticipatory.

Back to *your* business now. This creates a challenge: customers will compare you to this ever-more-convenient, ever-more-personally customized world every time they return to do business with you.

Therefore, any business that doesn't frequently update its own customer experience will start to seem creaky, slow, outdated, and out of touch compared to everything else your customer encounters in the outside world. This can be true even if, just recently, those same customers found the experience you provided entirely up-to-date.

Let's look at these changes in your customers' daily lives, and how such changes might affect their perception of your offerings and services.

It used to be that every car in the market required the driver to physically turn a key in the ignition, both to start the engine and as a way to prove that the person in the driver's seat was authorized to drive it. Now, it's more likely that the car knows who the driver is as they approach it—knows this in some detail, in fact. It knows how far back and at what angle the driver (and passengers) like to sit, how the mirrors should be adjusted, and more. And the vehicle will nonintrusively go through its security paces as well, to make sure that this driver is really supposed to be at the wheel, no key insertion necessary.

Then, as the driver pulls the car up to the gas pump, they don't even need to insert their credit card with the stripe on the correct side anymore. Card readers at most gas pumps will accept a card presented in any conceivable way—stripe on left, stripe on right, just tapping or waving it, or even as digits embedded in a smartphone's software. The gas pump *anticipates* the distraction of the average credit card-wielding customer and makes allowances for it.

And if it's summer, and the heat hovering in the air as the driver fills the gas tank gives them a hankering for a venti iced latte, they can order from their phone via the Starbucks app where the data in the app anticipates the flavoring and milk choices this particular customer is likely to want, the payment method they prefer to use, and so forth. In that way, a friendly Starbucks employees can have the highly personalized drink ready when the driver arrives at the store.*

Then, when your customer gets home and calls their pharmacy for a prescription refill, the pharmacy will know who is calling, whether any refills remain on the prescription in question, whether insurance will accept responsibility for payment, and more. The pharmacy accomplishes all this thanks to a databank that's pulled up by caller ID, which links the caller's phone number to a powerful back office full of extremely personal data. No need for a caller to identify themself manually, provide a paper prescription, or go through any of the traditional hassle customers used to accept as inevitable.

Now, it's not that such modernizations of the customer experience necessarily make a customer *consciously* love their new car more than the old one of blessed memory, or get excited about the experience of being able to present their credit card every which way at the gas pump, or become a vocal booster of the tech prowess of Big Latte or Big Pharmacy. However, if the accepted customer experience standards of, say, 2015 were to rear their aged heads in any of these scenarios, it would be jarring—and perhaps enough of an irritant to prompt an otherwise loyal customer to start searching for a more up-to-date, less taxing experience.

To avoid ending up on your customer's cutting-room floor,† you'll want to update the customer experience you provide

---

* Your safety-minded author wishes he could remind this hypothetical customer not to still be fiddling with their phone once they're back behind the wheel.

† Oops—that's a rapidly aging film-era reference. I tell you, it's an ongoing struggle to stay up-to-date!

with some frequency. And an effective way to make this happen is to include everyone in your organization in the pursuit of innovation, letting them know that, starting today, innovative suggestions will be *welcomed* as part of every employee's work, rather than being treated as interruptions.

That's an easy sentiment to write down, but for most companies it represents a cultural shift that will be challenging to achieve. The push for innovation needs to flow (or at least have solid support) from top leadership and be supported throughout all levels of your organization. This represents a big change from the status quo at many organizations, where employees with bright ideas are seen as time wasters at best and troublemakers at worst.

Steps to Set You on the Way Toward an Innovation Culture

If you're ready to start down the path toward creating an innovation culture, here are my suggestions.

Make Sure Everyone in Your Company Is Aware of *All Three* Areas Where You Seek Innovation

There are at least three types of innovation that you want people to be on the lookout for:

▶ **Product:** what you sell or make; in spite of the name, this includes services as well as goods.
▶ **Process:** how you make your product or service and how you sell it.

▶ **Business model:** how your company is conceptualized and organized.

The first of these three, product innovation, is invariably the one that grabs the headlines. That's why it's important to make clear that you're looking for innovation in the areas of process and business model as well.

Tamp Down on Any "Gotcha" Elements in Your Culture and Embrace the Openness to Look Silly

If it's safer in your company to support how things are right now than to suggest improvements, then the status quo is going to remain stubbornly in place. Innovative experimentation requires an openness to look silly in the short run as well as to risk actual failure in the longer run. If neither is considered acceptable in your company's culture, then innovation isn't going to happen.

Capture and Review Every Innovation Suggestion in a Systematic Way

Innovation is more than employees musing, "Gee, wouldn't it be great if . . .". That's actually a good start, but it won't get your organization far without a well-defined framework for receiving such ideas and giving them more than a perfunctory review. Employees will only contribute their innovative insights if they can be sure they'll be listened to and given the consideration they deserve.

And whoa! If you do set up such a framework and process, be ready for the floodgates to open. One company with a clear and transparent innovation process is USAA, the insurance and financial services giant. At USAA, every suggestion made through its innovation portal is logged, reviewed, and either acted on or responded to with well-considered commentary explaining the decision *not* to pursue it.

The result? USAA has generated *nearly 1,000 patents* based on employee suggestions.

Also look (again) to the example of Ace Hardware, which runs and promotes an Ace "Makers Portal" (innovatewithace .com) for both internal and external innovators to share their ideas as well as receive input on products that aren't quite ready for the market. Everything is tracked and reviewed in an organized, transparent manner. In addition, Ace builds excitement and visibility for innovation via events such as their Maker Convention and their partnership with Grommet (thegrommet.com), a company that specializes in teasing out and nurturing innovative products from entrepreneurs and small businesses. (Grommet's discoveries to date include Fitbit, Mrs. Meyer's Clean Day, and SodaStream.)

When an Innovation Succeeds in One Corner of Your Operation, Help It Spread to the Others

Getting the most, companywide, out of every innovation can be a major win, and it's more likely to occur if there is a system set up to review and spread localized successes you've had in one department, business unit, or location. Encourage (or even require) the submission of such locally successful ideas with the promise that they will be promptly reviewed and considered across the board.

Consider the Ritz-Carlton Hotel Company's System for Spreading Successful Innovations Companywide

Here's a ready-made system you can borrow (they won't mind) from the iconic Ritz-Carlton Hotel Company for spreading innovations from one part of an organization to anywhere else in the organization they could be useful.

Their approach is rock-solid, because it has to be. With more than 100 properties worldwide, in a wide variety of locations and situations, the Ritz-Carlton has a particularly strong need to make sure that successful new innovations practices spread companywide.

If a Ritz-Carlton employee at, say, its downtown Tokyo hotel comes up with a spectacularly more effective—or even just subtly better—way to handle, say, front desk staffing for peak check-in times, it would be a loss indeed to limit that improvement to a single hotel when the same challenge is also coming up at a hotel 4,740 miles away in Dubai.

That's where the Ritz-Carlton's innovation database comes in. There are, at present, more than 1,000 innovative practices in this database. Each of these practices is tested at a single hotel property before being added.

Here's a simple example: If one of Ritz-Carlton's oceanside resorts has the idea of putting those puffy beach tires on a delivery vehicle to facilitate beverage service for guests relaxing on the beach, that property's general manager can add this idea to the innovation database. Now, any other oceanside property looking for ideas to speed up their own beachside beverage service can look in the database and discover this tested, ready-made solution.

A significant point: Use of the database *is not optional*. To the contrary, over the course of a year, every hotel is instructed to submit at least seven such ideas to the database and select at least four ideas from other properties to help address its own challenges.

To avoid allowing the database to turn into a free-for-all or generic brainstorming receptacle, there are three requirements which a contribution must meet before it can be submitted. First, the idea needs to have been tested for at least three months to prove its value. Second, the contribution should advance the Ritz-Carlton Hotel Company's overall company goals and be consistent with its company principles. Finally, a contribution must be applicable to other properties, rather than so unique to one hotel's situation that it has no chance of working elsewhere (The vehicle with special tires would be of interest to other beach properties, so it passes this requirement.)

Build Breathing Space into Your Employees' Workday

When a company or department is chronically understaffed, with employees who are overworked and KPI'd (Key Performance Indicatored) to death regarding call lengths and the like and barely have time to think for themselves (or even, it seems, breathe), it's hard for employees to ever find the time (or motivation!) to involve themselves in innovation. For your organization to provide the best customer experience *today*, while building, via innovation, a better one for *tomorrow*, breathing space (created via sufficient staffing, sufficient breaks, and so forth) is essential.

Embrace and Promote an Attitude of "Honor Thy Mistakes"

This principle, formulated as "honor thy error as a hidden intention," was proposed years ago by musical innovator Brian Eno (you know him for cowriting and producing "Once in a Lifetime" for Talking Heads) and multimedia artist Peter Schmidt for one of their Oblique Strategies cards; it remains an effective way to improve. Some of the best innovations come from serendipitous accidents rather than linear progression. Encourage your team to embrace these accidental discoveries and apparent missteps, rather than disregarding them merely because they were unintended (or, as Eno and Schmidt suggest, subconsciously intended).

Embrace Negativity (Sort of)

Certainly, you want to employ positive people, particularly in customer-facing roles. But encouraging an attitude of "everything is fine the way it is, and we should all be happy with the status quo—and so, by the way, should our customers" will squelch innovation. A "we only want good news" attitude will render your company a sitting duck for more innovative competitors to set their sights on, competitors who figure out that your current way of doing business is less perfect than your Pollyanna attitude may assume.

Also Involve Your *Customers* in Innovation

Involving your customers in innovation has a double value. Not only will you obtain insights from customers due to their distinct viewpoint, you'll increase buy-in from those same customers after they've involved themselves in your innovation process. Today's customers enjoy collaborating with businesses and brands—as long as they believe that what they say matters to the company in question. They don't necessarily see a clear boundary between their role as customer and the brands they patronize. Embrace this modern reality!

Use Technology to Harvest Unintentional and Unsolicited Customer and Employee Contributions

Technology such as the CallMiner Eureka product and the line of offerings from Authenticx can facilitate automatic call recording and transcription, "listening" to every call, incoming and outbound, and converting the words exchanged on those calls into structured data. This is a great way to bubble up insights from customers, prospects, and employees.

And, at least once, its power has been used to prevent a customer's home from erupting into flames.

One CallMiner client is a leading provider of gaming consoles. In an initial review of call transcriptions, words such as "smoke" and "fire" kept appearing with surprising regularity. The executives in the room initially assumed these were references to plot points in a game, or that maybe the game was so great it was "smoking" and "on fire"!

However, a closer read revealed a frantic gamer who'd had to rush out of his house and into the street when smoke began to pour out of his console! And additional analyses showed that this wasn't an isolated incident. Happily, the manufacturer was able to identify the problem quickly and proactively resolve it before any harm was done and before it hit the media, social or otherwise.

This is obviously a rare sort of case, but you'll be surprised at the variety of insights you can gain from this method—even if you never have the opportunity to prevent a customer's house from burning to the ground.

Spare Your People the Agony of Staring Down a Blank Page

It's a slog when potential innovators have to start from absolute scratch, trying to fill an oppressively blank sheet of paper. A great way around this is to share innovation prompts with everybody. (This is similar in concept to the writing prompts you may have encountered in school.) Here's my list of 25 prompts to help your organization get the innovation juices flowing.

MICAH SOLOMON'S 25 PROMPTS FOR SPARKING INNOVATION

1. **Borrow a concept from nature.** Think caterpillars metamorphosing into butterflies, owls seeing at night, or, for historical inspiration, the humble mouse that became an essential adjunct to the graphic user interface (GUI). And even though earthworms cut in half can't *actually* regenerate from both pieces, that we want it to be true shows that it's a concept that— ahem—has legs.

2. **Channel a particular visionary or vision.** Take your product or service and Jony Ive (Apple) it or Frank Lloyd Wright it or RuPaul it. You'd be surprised how many perspective swaps like this are already part of our cultural and commercial landscape. To wit: even though we consider Bambi to be as American as French fries (!), it in fact drew its distinctive look from ancient Chinese art.

3. **Take an approach from another industry.** What would Starbucks do? Cleveland Clinic? Harley Davidson? Looking to companies in industries far afield is a great way to freshen up your thinking. It's also a source for ideas you might be able to borrow, add a little twist to, and go to town.

4. **Try the *opposite* of your normal approach or look for opportunities at the other end of the process.** You're trying to be the cheapest provider, but what would the premium version look like? Right now, you *sell* diapers, but the diaper market is, uh, saturated. So, how about diaper *disposal*?

5. **Evoke a different emotion.** Maybe you are selling on fear when you should be selling on hope. Or vice versa.

6. **Change the terms.** Rent vs. buy, long-term vs. short-term, and so on. Disney successfully got people to "invest" in DVD and Blu-ray long after these formats were on the road to obsolescence, while Netflix, Audible, and many others have succeeded by promoting a subscription model, where nothing is owned or even, by and large, rented.

7. **Change the timing.** Sell them breakfast when you were previously only open for lunch and dinner (McDonald's). Promote health club membership purchases in August instead of around the New Year. Ask customers to join your loyalty program at a different moment in their relationship with you. Offer passengers a drink while the plane is still languishing on the ground, rather than waiting until mid-flight.

8. **Invent or embrace off-label uses.** Think up new uses for your existing product or embrace the ways that customers are *already* using your product that differ from your original intention. A morally dubious, but financially triumphant, example of the latter is the success that Pedialyte—initially intended as an electrolyte replacement for sick kids (hence the "pedia" in its name)—has had by embracing the use of its product by hard-partying adults. This came about after its maker, Abbott Laboratories, noticed that social media "authorities" were raving online about using Pedialyte as a hangover cure.

9. **Combine existing elements.** Early smartphones weren't particularly great phones (sound-wise) or cameras (quality-wise). However, the *combination* of

features—the ability to have your camera everywhere your phone is, and to have it connected to the rest of humanity, changed the world.

10. **Remove features.** Do your customers actually want the smorgasbord of features you're including, or do they feel, rightly or wrongly, that your generosity in this regard means they're paying for features they never use?

11. **Add features.** Maybe your product or service doesn't include everything your customers want. What's missing?

12. **Do what you already do, but in a different medium.** Substituting voice recognition for keyboard input is essential to the magic trick effect of Siri, Alexa, and similar systems.

13. **Add humor.** Ben & Jerry's, Virgin brands, and others have thrived by embracing humor—an element that is lacking in much of the commercial world. When you buy from Moosejaw, a seller of outdoor clothing, you're likely to receive a repurposed package—perhaps a previously used FedEx overnight pouch turned inside out—that says, "NO KNIFE, USE TEETH." Believe me, this packaging innovation gets attention (while putting a smile on customers' faces); in fact, little innovations like this put the company, which was founded by four camping enthusiasts, on track for its eventual acquisition by Walmart for $51 million.

14. **Add nostalgia.** The Hanx Writer, an app that turns your modern mobile device into an old-school typewriter complete with clanking keys and retro sounds when you "return the carriage," is an adorable example (courtesy of Tom Hanks) of this approach.

15. **Pay attention to a neglected part of your offering.** Think of how Tiffany & Co. took a mundane aspect of its product (the packaging) and made the blue box central to the Tiffany experience and brand.

16. **Strive to turn your product or service into a habit or ritual.** Ronald McDonald House Charities created a charitable donation ritual by adding a donation box right under the drive-thru windows of McDonald's restaurants. And now, in our nearly cashless society, they're again striving to create a new ritual of giving via their "Round up for Ronald McDonald House" program, which works with any type of payment and at their drive-thru windows, self-order kiosks, or on their app.

17. **Involve the crowd.** When you involve your customers, not only do you get the value of their wisdom, but you can also endear your brand to them through the *IKEA effect.* This is the observation that customers place greater value on products they have had a hand in creating (or, in IKEA's case, assembling).

18. **Make it self-service.** Some customers want to do everything for themselves. And I mean *everything.* So, it's possible that your product offering may never appeal to this cohort until you remove the human interaction element. Try a self-service option and see if things take off.

19. ***Resist* making it self-service.** Singapore Airlines *intentionally* designed the seats in its international business class cabins to require flight attendant intervention when a passenger is ready to use their lie-flat bed. The airline could have made this feature automatic or self-service (as it is on other carriers) with the bedding already in place or in a luggage bin nearby,

to be used whenever the passenger is ready. But the airline opted for inserting a human touchpoint here and set things up so that a flight attendant needs to interact with you when it's bedtime. (This isn't a right or wrong choice until customers deem it one way or the other, so give it a try and see how it works out.)

20. **Add a social element.** The 1888 hotel in Sydney could be just another hotel (a nice one, actually), but it has turned itself into a magnet for Instagram enthusiasts by mapping out which properties and neighborhoods are best for photo ops. (It's also placed a gigantic, human-sized picture frame in its lobby). If you think about it, you'll find your own ways (more subtle, perhaps) to socialize your offering to extend and improve the appeal of your product or service.

21. **Make it smaller.** Some things become more valuable when you miniaturize them or make them portable, such as laptops vs. desktops, tablets vs. laptops, and wearables vs. handheld devices.

22. **Make the user base bigger.** Some products or services only work if a critical mass of customers is already using them. This was the initial sticking point back in the day for fax machines and even, *way* back in the day (I've been told), for telephones: they were of limited utility until there were enough other people to fax with, or, much earlier, to talk to on the phone. So maybe your goal should be to first build up a large network of users, as opposed to trying to make all your income from a small group of early adopters.

23. **Explain it better.** Maybe you don't need to rework your product itself. Maybe all you need is a three-minute

video to orient new users so they don't sour on your product due to their initial confusion.

24. **Solve something everyone else has accepted as the way things are.** This may be the most classic innovation prompt of all time and it's still a great one, sparking those "they said it couldn't be done!" innovations.

25. **Accept rather than solve, but *monetize* that acceptance.** Some movie theaters have reacted to theatergoer complaints about (other) audience members bringing babies to regular showings at the theater by scheduling separate showings where parents and babies are not only tolerated, but expected and invited.

Free resource for readers: For a formatted, printable, shareable copy of my **25 *Innovation Prompts***, simply email me at **micah@micahsolomon.com** and I'll get it right out to you.

CUSTOMER SERVICE EXCELLENCE IS A MOVING TARGET

How to Build a Culture of Innovation

As more and more products, services, and businesses out there incorporate anticipatory aspects, it's important to keep updating your own customer experience. What was cutting edge a few months ago may seem outdated tomorrow.

There are three areas where you should be encouraging innovation in your organization:

- **Product:** what you sell or make
- **Process:** how you make it/how you sell it
- **Business model:** how your company is conceptualized and organized

Of these, product innovation is the one that grabs the headlines, so it's particularly useful to clarify, companywide, that process and business model innovations are valued as well.

Ways to Stay Ahead of the Curve

Invite and Encourage Suggestions

Let your staff know that you are open to their innovative ideas. Make sure your staff feels support from you in the quest for innovation.

Here are seven tips that will help you harvest innovative ideas from your employees:

1. Make sure all innovation suggestions are logged, reviewed, and either acted on or responded to in a way that explains why an idea won't be pursued at this time.
2. Ensure your employees feel safe and encouraged in making suggestions.
3. If an idea works well in one department or at one location, see if it can translate to other areas of your business as well.
4. Give your employees enough breathing space to step away from their routine and think about ways to innovate.
5. Embrace mistakes. Sometimes the best ideas come from accidents.
6. Look to your *customers* as well for innovative ideas.
7. Use technology to gather *unsolicited* and *unintentional* innovation ideas from your customers and employees on recorded and transcribed phone calls.

(continued)

Innovation Prompts

It can be hard to think of ideas when you're staring at a blank page. To improve on this situation, consider making use of, from earlier in this chapter, the 25 Prompts to Spark Innovation.

Free resource for readers: For a formatted, printable, shareable copy of Micah's *25 Prompts to Spark Innovation*, simply email micah@micahsolomon.com and I'll get it right out to you. Please, to satisfy my curiosity, tell me a little about yourself, your company, and your situation.

CHAPTER 12

MAKE IT STICK

Secrets of Effective Standards Setting and Customer Service Training

I f you and I were to work together on a customer service transformation initiative, we'd make valuable progress together; I have little doubt.

And though we're not working face-to-face, I appreciate you taking this journey with me by way of the printed word. I want to encourage you in particular to read, review, and take to heart this upcoming chapter, as I've poured into it everything I can to help you on your way toward undertaking a customer service initiative on your own (you won't *really* be your own, since you have this book—and me!).

This chapter focuses on two "success components" to sustain you on your journey toward iconic customer service status. These components fall broadly into two areas:

1. Creating and deploying customer service **standards**
2. Developing and deploying customer service **training**

Let's take these one by one.

Success Component 1:
Develop and Deploy Service Standards

Breakdowns in the customer service experience are rarely the result of bad employees hellbent on doing dumb things. More often, they're due to a lack of customer service standards spelling out the expected behavior and course of action that would have prevented the breakdown in the first place.

Standards, and groups of standards (which we could also call *frameworks* or *systems*), work behind the scenes to create and sustain customer service excellence. I've already provided many standards in this book, including standards for language, correspondence, surveys, telephone conversations, and service recovery. And in the pages that follow, I'll show you how to construct standards for yourself that will go a long way toward supporting exceptional customer service on a consistent and sustainable basis.

Although customer service should *appear* natural, even effortless, to the customer, there's more to the story. As a professional, you need to understand that successfully serving customers relies on more than smiles (although smiles are important). It leans heavily on the creation, dissemination, and enforcement of standards that will allow you to consistently provide great service, day in and day out.

A hotel is a particularly good exemplar of how a standards-rich institution should operate. A hotel will have dozens of standards guiding its guest service in a very broad range of situations. For example, a hotel will have standards for parking valets in order to telegraph enthusiasm and interest at this important arrival and departure point (including, traditionally, that the valet *run*, or at least walk briskly, rather than saunter up to the customer cars they are there to park) as well as related standards for how to handle a guest's car (don't change the radio station or the driver's seat position, and so forth).

Companies in other industries will benefit from having defined standards that are similar, but relevant to their own context and customer set. Here are two examples from very disparate industries.

Take *automotive retailing*. A car dealership might want to set a standard of accompanying every arriving customer on foot from their car to the service desk, holding an umbrella for them if necessary.

In *healthcare*, a standard (that is both good service and good medicine) could require that a health provider, before proceeding to administer medication, ask each patient to state their own name aloud rather than just answering—or nodding in apparent answer to—a leading question. Consider how much better it is to adhere to a script such as,

> *"Before I administer this medicine, can you please tell me your name and date of birth?*

(a question like this requires an active answer, eliminating an opportunity for a potentially catastrophic misidentification), instead of,

> *"I'm going to give you your medicine now—you're Mrs. Ogilvy, correct?"*

(an approach that requires only a head nod or "uh huh" from a maybe groggy and tuned-out patient who, if she is not in fact Mrs. Ogilvy, may experience a dangerous reaction*).

---

* And the actual Mrs. Ogilvy may never get her medication to boot!

How to Construct a Standard

When working to create new standards, it's useful to do a three-part write-up for each standard. This will clarify your own thinking and document your ideas for posterity. (The *public* version of the service standard, the one that will be referenced on a day to day basis within your company, may be more brief and to the point than this three-part writeup, but it's still an important exercise.)

These are the three points you should consider for every new standard:

▶ The standard itself
▶ Why the standard is of value
▶ The response (typically an emotion) you're aiming to evoke in your customer*

Reviewing each potential standard validates your thinking and clarifies your intention. And, later on, it can help (if you keep your paperwork around) to determine if the standard no longer makes sense: if it no longer provides the value (bullet point two) or no longer triggers the intended customer response (bullet point three), then you know it's time to tweak or eliminate it entirely. (Think of how in its early days as a modern company the Ritz-Carlton used to "my pleasure" its guests almost to the point of exhaustion. Some years down the road, the hotel company determined that this wording no longer achieved the emotive goal of "comfort and a touch of class" [I'm paraphrasing] that was initially intended, so they backed off on its use; even though it had clearly become something of a brand trademark, it was failing its initial purpose.)

Here are examples of this three-part write-up. I'll base these on standards I've already shared with you in Chapters 8 and 9.

---

* Note that the content in items 2 and 3 are likely to have some overlap.

Constructing Telephone Communication Standards

1. **Our standard:** We answer the telephone within three rings (in other words, prior to the fourth ring).

   The reasoning behind this standard: When a caller has to wait beyond three rings it's been shown to breed customer anxiety and doubt.

   The customer response this standard aims to achieve: A feeling of comfort and a belief in our company's ability to serve their needs.

2. **Our standard:** We only screen incoming calls if truly necessary, in which case we do so minimally and politely, implying immediately that the caller *will* get through, rather than challenging them for their credentials.

   The reasoning behind this standard: We want to avoid making a caller feel they have to prove themselves in order to talk with us. Challenging a caller with questions like, "What is the nature of your call?" is the polar opposite of being hospitable.

   The customer response this standard aims to achieve: To ensure the caller feels *welcomed* from the moment they interact with us on the phone.

3. **Our standard:** We identify ourselves personally when we pick up the phone.

   The reasoning behind this standard: Callers like to feel they have a way to circle back to the person they first spoke with should that ever become necessary. Plus, by offering our names, we correct what would be an asymmetry of information: we have, or will soon have, information on the caller's identity; it's only reasonable to share ours in return.

The customer response this standard aims to achieve: The caller should feel that an individual human being at our company is "in their court" from the moment they begin to interact with us.

Constructing Standards for Written Correspondence

1. **Our standard:** Every piece of correspondence (email or printed) will include the name of the correspondent and a *direct* way to reach them.

   The reasoning behind this standard: When we send out any piece of correspondence, no matter how mundane, we are putting a demand on the recipient's time. So, if the recipient should desire anything from *us*, they deserve a way to reach us as directly as possible.

   The customer response this standard aims to achieve: The feeling that *we are easy to do business with and available should they ever need anything,* whether or not their need is related to the specific piece of correspondence they've received.

2. **Our standard:** We include details and attachments that the recipient will benefit from, whether they've thought to request these details, while being careful not to overload them with extraneous materials.

   The reasoning behind this standard: This is part of our overarching principle of striving to be anticipatory and to reach beyond explicitly stated desires and questions. When a customer requests something of us, whether in writing or otherwise, we—being the experts—should strive to thoroughly answer the request. This means including anything useful to the recipient that, although never spelled out as a request, may be helpful to them nonetheless.

The customer response this standard aims to achieve:
A feeling of comfort and assistance when they read our correspondence as well as, later on, when they engage in whatever action it ultimately facilitates.

Success Component 2: Customer Service Training

The HOW: How Should Customer Service Training Be Delivered?

The training landscape has been changing quickly, so I'll start with a discussion of *how* to deploy training—the methods that work best—before getting to the even more essential *what*: what training content you should be sure to cover.

Training Option 1 – eLearning: Even if, up to this point, you've exclusively relied on doing everything live and in person, I encourage you to consider the value of having someone build a custom, exclusive to your company's situation, eLearning customer service training program (such as—you know I'd be foolish not to mention this!—what my company is known for). eLearning should be tailored to the specifics of your company; your business isn't generic and your training shouldn't be, either. eLearning (done right) can be a uniquely powerful and convenient platform for training in any organization, offering the opportunity for asynchronous learning that doesn't require everyone to train in the same place and at the same time. (Although, if you prefer, it can be used in a classroom setting for concurrent learning and the opportunity to have a training facilitator assist.)

The joke around the office here* is that eLearning is valuable because its usability lasts long after, Elvis-style, "Micah has left the building." In other words, it can be used for years to follow and be incorporated as part of your onboarding for future employees. eLearning can include *progress measurements* that allow for employee growth as well as *certification* upon completion.

**Micah Solomon delivering
customer service training via eLearning.**

---

* If you want to learn more about our customer service training offerings, and why we make this Elvis-inspired joke, you can learn more about at **www .micahsolomon.com** or by sending me an email at **training@micahsolomon .com**. In your email, please let me know a bit about your situation, company, and anything else you think I'd find interesting and helpful in responding!

Training Option 2 – Live, in-person (classroom) training and training facilitation: In-person training is of course the classic delivery channel for training. It can be used exclusively, or in concert with eLearning, if your approach is structured properly. As you are unique, your live training should be as well. It should be customized for your company, industry, and situation.

The WHAT: What Should Your Customer Service Training Include, and How Should It Be Framed and Focused?

1. **Your customer service training should be framed in a way that puts your *organizational purpose* (see Chapter 3) front and center.** While the nitty-gritty, nuts-and-boltsy, best practices parts of training are of course essential, your training should also be sure to emphasize how all of this is being done in service of the organizational purpose you determined back in Chapter 3.

   Here are three industry-specific examples of purpose-centered training:

   - **Customer service training for a retail store** might center on "becoming the most customer-focused operation in retail [or, more specifically, luxury retail or economy minded retail or sporting goods sales, etc.]" and include the concepts and practical aspects necessary to live up to this ideal, from gold-touch customer service to improving phone, in-person, and email interactions to building a default of yes to the MAMA method of service recovery.

- **Guest service training for a hotel or resort** might be designed to serve a purpose such as (and this is an actual one from Fairmont Hotels and Resorts), "turning moments into memories," attaching to this purposeful framework the concepts and practical aspects required to make this happen daily, interaction by interaction.
- **A patient experience training program in healthcare** could be informed by an idea along the lines of the primary stated value of Mayo Clinic ("the needs of the patient come first") and strive to make this statement come alive through every interaction with patients and their loved ones.

2. **Include training for situational empathy.** *Situational empathy* is the type of empathy that nearly every employee can learn to exhibit.* If you train employees in situational empathy, they'll be developing the mindset and skillset to react and respond appropriately toward a wide variety of customers they'll encounter on the job.

   You can think about situational empathy training as solving for the barriers that get in the way of your employees being empathetic. One of these common barriers is when customer-facing employees haven't ever experienced the situation in which a customer finds themselves in and may be struggling to convey.

---

* It's distinct from empathy as a personality trait, which is a good thing because it means you don't limit yourself to only hiring people who have been psychologically built a particular way.

Case in point: In the healthcare system, the employees who answer the phones and schedule appointments may not have had a personal experience similar to what the patient on the other end of the phone line (who's very likely apprehensive and may even be in pain) is up against. These schedulers often work out of a separate, nonclinical building and are therefore unlikely to encounter even a single patient face-to-face while on the job. And sometimes, if they're fortunate and/or quite young, they may have never even set foot inside a healthcare facility outside of the office of their family doctor.

How can you bridge this disconnect? The training solution I recommend is to simulate clinical moments using role playing and video, to provide an inkling of how it feels to be a patient. (This is one place where eLearning has an advantage, as scripted video-based scenarios can be a powerful way to arouse empathy. These can be paired with prompting from a live training facilitator as well, as indicated.)

Another stumbling block is the challenge involved in recognizing that time may move differently for the customer than it does for the employee. Training on this topic and role-playing can help cue employees to the customer's pacing and help them understand how a customer's external realities may make a situation more urgent for them than it may seem to the employee. (To use a healthcare example again, but this time from within the hospital, when a patient is in pain, or is feeling the pressure of a full bladder, they may experience the wait time for relief as much longer than it seems to a busy care provider.)

In addition to the above discussion about *creating* situational empathy, there are many ways to train your employees in *conveying* empathy.

Many of these cues have already been covered in the previous sections of this book, from which you can draw your training materials:

- The discussion of the power of recognition (Chapter 4)
- The first three steps of the MAMA framework for service recovery: **M**ake time to listen; **A**cknowledge and, if it's called for, apologize; and Have a **M**eeting of minds (Chapter 5)
- The entire language chapter, including the discussion on replacing defensive language with neutral (Chapter 6)

In addition, here are a few specifics to keep in mind as you plan and populate your training for situational empathy:

- **Encourage employees to reframe before every customer interaction.** When an employee has had 45 similar calls, it's important that they have the right frame of mind going into call 46—that this call, even if it seems rote to them, is going to be a unique experience for the caller, for better or worse. This reframing will cut down on employees rushing customers, using shorthand, or becoming jaded—or at least from *sounding* jaded.
- **Train employees to avoid anything nonverbal that may come across as dismissive.** The physician

whose hand is on the outgoing doorknob while a patient is still asking questions is a classic example.

3. **Include training for service recovery** (at length— it's so important) and for **the types of interactions employees are likely to engage in with customers.** This may include telephone engagements, digital communication (emails, texts, webchats, etc.), or in-person interactions.

Seven Secrets for Making Customer Service Training More Powerful– and Making Its Lessons Stick

1. **Have your department head, or even your CEO,* attend the training (or at least the kickoff to the training) and have them introduce the session.** If you want make it clear to employees that your organization cares about customer service, convince someone high within your organization to attend and even introduce the training.

2. **Provide printed† support material for attendees to keep them on the same page after the training.** For decades, the Ritz-Carlton Hotel Company has kept every employee *literally* on the same (tiny) page by providing them with an accordion-folded pocket card

---

* Sound unrealistic? At the Ritz-Carlton Hotel Company, all its executives, up to and including its president, are known for attending trainings, particularly when a hotel is opened or re-opened as a Ritz-Carlton, no matter where in the world that new hotel is located. Jetlag is not considered an executive excuse.

† Or if your workforce is distributed, *printable*.

that they can refer to any time they need a refresher. The card, in fact, is considered part of an employee's uniform.

3. **Certify attendees when they complete the training.** Attendees appreciate when a training, in-person or virtual, concludes with something tangible. For this reason, my company's training programs include a colorful, personalized certificate of completion to show that the employee attended—and succeeded in showing tangible progress at—the session. Our certificates aren't overly fancy, but they are frame-worthy. And if you can spring for modestly priced, mountable frames—such as the ones that always seem to be on sale at Target—it will complete the picture.

A typical certificate of completion from one of our eLearning courses. The one pictured is customized for a golfing retailer's training program.

4. **The onboarding (orientation) experience for new employees should have customer service front and center.** At some companies, what could have been a meaningful orientation has been overshadowed by dictums from the legal department, loss prevention, and so on. These are no doubt important, but also make a point to stress the seriousness with which your company takes its pro-customer mission and how central that mission is to the work the new employees attending orientation will be carrying out.

5. **Celebrate great customer service moments when they happen, as well as at scheduled intervals.** These can be as simple as the ad hoc posting of thank-you letters on the office's physical or virtual bulletin board. But I suggest you *systematize* the celebration, along the lines of what has worked for years—decades—at the Ritz-Carlton Hotel Company. On Monday and Friday, every Ritz-Carlton hotel and resort shares a "wow story" from one of the brand's more than 100 properties to inspire employees to be similarly effective at creating "wow" and to, perhaps, have their own inspiring "wow story" shared companywide in the future.

6. **Supplement and sustain your training with the daily (or at least weekly) sustaining ritual I call the *customer service minute*,** which is a very brief customer service brushup session that's held frequently, ideally at all levels of your company. This is a way to make the lessons of customer service training not only last, but grow in power throughout the year. A customer service minute is a very short meeting (longer than a minute, in spite of its name, but shorter than 10 minutes), held

every single day. Or, if that's too frequent for your company, hold it once a week.

At each session, you'll want to focus on *just one* of your customer service principles and standards. I suggest that you ask a *different* nonmanagerial employee to prepare for and lead each session—or at least pass the leadership baton between hands every five meetings or so, to share the burden and allow more employees to learn by teaching. Consider this: over the course of a year, the customer service minute approach allows you to pay a stupendous amount of attention to every aspect of customer service excellence.

7. **Walk the walk.** Any time an employee sees someone in senior management assisting or warmly greeting a customer, it's a strong reinforcement.

* * *

Free resource for readers (be sure take me up on this one!): As a benefit to you, my readers, email me directly at micah@micahsolomon.com for a copy of these customer service training principles in a printable format. Put something like "training principles, please" in the subject line and, if you have a minute, *please* tell me a little bit about yourself and your organization.

MAKE IT STICK

Make It Stick: Secrets of Effective Standards Setting and Customer Service Training

---

This chapter was a look at how to sustain a company and its employees on the journey toward customer service excellence, focusing on two "success components."

Success Component I: Develop and Deploy Customer Service Standards

Although customer service should *appear* effortless, you need a rigorous set of standards behind the scenes to guide employees in delivering superior service.

Many of These Standards Have Already Been Touched Upon in Earlier Chapters of This Book

- Language
- Written correspondence
- Telephone interactions
- Service recovery

(continued)

Constructing a New Standard

When constructing a new standard, be sure to think through these three points:

- The standard itself (what is prescribed to be done from here forward)
- Why this standard is of value (why we do it)
- The response, often an emotion, we're aiming to evoke in the customer

Success Component II: Customer Service Training

Your employees need training—the right kind of training—to become experts in the art of delivering exceptional customer service.

Training can be delivered either in person or via an eLearning package.

What should be included in your customer service training?

- Your customer service training should be framed in a way that puts your purpose front and center, while also covering the nuts and bolts of desired behaviors.
- Training for situational empathy.
- Training for service recovery and for types of interactions employees are likely to engage in: telephone engagements, digital (emails, texts, webchats) and in-person interactions in all their variety.

Seven Secrets to Make Customer Service Training More Powerful—and Make the Lessons Stick

1. Have your department head or CEO attend the training (or at least the kickoff) and provide an introduction to the session. This sends a powerful message about the training's importance.
2. Give employees supporting resources, probably printed, to retain for future reference.
3. Certify attendees with an official certificate of completion.
4. Move customer service to the forefront of the onboarding experience for new employees.
5. Celebrate customer service triumphs companywide.
6. Offer a daily (or weekly) "customer service minute," a very brief meeting focusing on just one customer service principle each session.
7. Walk the walk. When employees catch their leaders delivering great customer service themselves, it reinforces everything they've learned during training.

AFTERWORD

Thanks for spending this time with me!
I hope to hear from you if I can help.

I've had the time of my life writing this book for you, and I hope you've had a grand time as well. And, more importantly, found the kind of information and inspiration that will serve you now and from here forward.

Any book like this is necessarily aimed at a general, hypothetical reader. But you are an actual, specific human being in a business situation like no other. So, if you want help with a specific scenario or situation, I, along with my team, am available to you, either informally or professionally. I answer my own texts, email, and phone (if you're not a spammer). I even personally handle the live chat on my website, although it's getting harder and harder to convince people on live chat that I'm not actually a bot!

Most of all, I hope this book has given you the tools to start and sustain your journey toward becoming a customer service legend. Many thanks for reading.

Micah Solomon   micah@micahsolomon.com
www.micahsolomon.com
(484) 343-5881

ACKNOWLEDGMENTS

First and most important: Thank you to my wife and family for giving me the time and space that made this book possible and the enjoyable interruptions that kept it from being a slog.

Second, thank you to my clients, present, past, and future!

Next, thank you to the team that helped directly to put this book together: legendary agent Bill Gladstone of Waterside Productions, editor extraordinaire Michele Matrisciani, Steve Straus of THINK Book Works, crackerjack researcher Jeanie Casison, Donya Dickerson, Scott McCormick, and the proofreading, copyediting, and production teams at McGraw Hill. Finally, thank you to graphic design—and everything else—wizard Jorge Krüger, video genius Ted Cumpston, and great friends and colleagues Ari Solomon, Matthias Debecki, Yaniv Masjedi, Cary and Deb Wheeland, Leonardo Inghilleri, Ann Alba, Portia Cook, Petra Kluge, David Pace, Blain Crandell, M.D., Slim and Brenda Harrison, Raj Singh, Bernie Thompson, Jayson Yardley, Lisa Holladay, Yaniv Masjedi, Peter Economy, Shawn Foley, Chirag Shah, M.D., Dan Schuman and Veer90, Seth Godin, Ed Miller, Rebecca Ravenal, Alison Sitch, Amine

Khechfe, Chris Reaburn, Tomas Gorny, Phil Steitz, Julie and Drew Toomey, Adam Cook, Tally McClain, Laura Romanoff, Deb Giffen, Jeroen Quint, Grace Sharples Cook, Colin Taylor, Daniel H. Pink, Seth Ferriell, Kent Bozarth, Joey Phelps, Rebecca Bartholomae, CPA, Girish Mathrubootham, Bill Quiseng, Adrian Swinscoe, Sam Patel, Bob Flanyak, David Seelinger, Daniel Hostettler, Micah Zimmerman ("the other Micah"), Seth Goldman, Kimberly Thompson and Panos Panay, Tue Søttrup, Nidhish Rajan, and the wonderful people I'm undoubtedly neglecting due to the limitations of my notes and memory.

INDEX

ABOUT THE AUTHOR

(Photo Credit: Danielle Barnum)

Micah Solomon, President and CEO of Four Aces, Inc., is a leading authority, consultant, author, speaker, trainer, and content creator on customer service, the customer experience, hospitality, and customer service culture. His bestselling books have been translated into more than a half-dozen languages and are the recipients of multiple awards. His expertise has been featured in *Forbes*, the *New York Times*, *Harvard Business Review*, the *Washington Post*, *Entrepreneur*, *Bloomberg Businessweek*, and many television networks and affiliates.

A business leader and entrepreneur himself, Micah built his own company into a market leader—a story that readers of Seth Godin's *Purple Cow* will be familiar with. He was an early investor in the technology behind Apple's Siri, and his broad expertise touches on technology, the hospitality industry, manufacturing, the automotive industry, banking, financial services, high-net-worth individuals (HNWIs), retail, the patient experience in healthcare, and the nonprofit and governmental sectors (federal, state, and local).

Through his consulting firm, Four Aces, Inc., Micah and his team are available to readers of this book in the following areas of professional practice:

- **Customer service transformation initiatives and customer service consulting**
- **Training and training design** (live and via custom-created eLearning)
- **Keynote speaking**
- **Book authorship/coauthorship/ghostwriting**
- **Content creation and influencer work**
- **Expert witness work** (practice limited to customer service and the customer experience)

You can reach Micah and team *right away* (seriously—try us!) via the following channels:

Email: micah@micahsolomon.com
Website: micahsolomon.com
Live chat: chat.micahsolomon.com
Text or voice: (484) 343-5881